TAROT
FOR BEGINNERS

HOW TO READ THE TAROT CARDS IN SEVEN SIMPLE STEPS

Unlock the Meaning of Each Major Tarot Card
and Discover the Answers to Love, Career,
and Life's Biggest Questions

YVES ROCHON

TABLE OF CONTENTS

BOOK 1

MAJOR ARCANA:
THE TAROT SERIES

"Above all, the Tarot is a guide for men and women searching for spiritual enlightenment who are determined to devote the necessary time and patience to discovering life's deeper meaning."

– COLETTE SILVESTRE

MY STORY

I was born in the beautiful Ottawa-Gatineau region at the start of spring in 1973. I was born at 11:11 a.m., dead, and my mother nearly died too. But by some miracle, we both survived.

When I was three, I had my first vision. Several years later, I discovered that it was of a guardian angel called 'The Gatekeeper'. Growing up, I was not like other children. I would see or dream about events before they happened. While other children experienced their lives in real time, I relived my dreams and visions.

My mother, who has always been spiritual, introduced me to tarot card reading, palmistry, and psychic development at a very young age. Before she passed away, my grandmother gave me her gift of card reading. Later, my friend Lorraine — whom I affectionately call my spiritual grandmother — introduced me to evolutionary astrology and tarot. All three of these important women in my life were born under the sign of Aquarius. I owe everything I am today to my maternal lineage.

In 1993, while working in a hospital, I had a very special vision. This time, I saw Christ. I received the following message telepathically:

"Honour your calling despite your setbacks. We are on this journey together, and I'm here to honour that journey."

I knew at that moment that my life would never be ordinary. I embarked on a long spiritual journey involving classes, training, regression, meditation, and channelling. In 2005, my masters required me to share my knowledge with others. To date, I am the author of three published books.

After a long dry spell and some surgeries, I struggled with depression rooted in not following my heart or the calling of my soul. Once again, I died, this time in the recovery room. The next day, I fell asleep in my rocking chair and my masters appeared again. Suddenly, I was surrounded by light in all its forms and it felt as though my DNA had been completely reshaped.

As they say, everything happens in threes. In 2009, a third apparition occurred during meditation. I found myself in front of a golden angel standing before golden doors. At first, I didn't understand what I was seeing. Its energy was so intense that I could not make out its features. I later realised it had none. The energy around it flowed like a curtain of light, like an aurora borealis dancing to a celestial symphony. The angel held a gilded book in its hands, its iridescent pages shimmering. Then, the word 'Akasha' appeared in bold letters.

For a few moments, I surrendered myself completely to the angel. Although I was blindfolded, I could feel a sensation as if I had wings curling up around me. I sensed those wings closing in on themselves. That's when I saw the golden book again. Its writing glowed with a heavenly, golden light, yet I could not decipher it. Despite the blindfold, I could see everything clearly.

Feeling calm and amazed, I questioned my inner light, seeking the meaning of this vision. The answer came: "It is time for you to stop procrastinating and letting yourself become destabilised by what happens around you. Your eyes are distracted. Let silence awaken from within. Now listen with your eyes and read what is written. You were born to see from within and read the invisible. What can you *hear* when you look at this sacred book?"

Suddenly, I felt my wings folding in around me like the horn of an old record player.

When I reflect on this vision, its rare intensity still gives me chills. I knew then that it was time to follow my soul's calling and become who I was always meant to be. It was a revelation of the purest kind. I was given the gift of being able to read people's souls and see their karmic issues, soul gifts, life mission and blockages from past lives, as well as how to heal them. With this gift came the opportunity to make a difference in the world and awaken as many people as possible, helping them to reconnect with their soul.

The purpose

The purpose of this book is to help people reconnect with their inner wisdom and, most importantly, discover their unique gifts. These teachings are drawn from my personal experience and extensive training. They are intended to empower readers with the tools they need to fulfil their life's mission.

The Reason

This book was created to provide readers with a variety of spiritual tools to help them gain a deeper understanding of themselves. I want to give them practical ways to discover who they are, where they have come from, and where they are going. I hope they will develop their intuition and learn how to manifest their dreams, among other things.

A Message of Hope

Having never felt that I fit in, I know how it feels to be different. People from all walks of life are searching for something meaningful — something deeper than what they experience in their daily lives. I am here to help them embrace and develop their gifts.

As a psychic astrologer and divine conduit for guides and angels, I am skilled in all eight clair senses, psychic art, past life regression, visions and Akashic record reading. I also have experience in channelling, tarot, astrology, numerology, healing, communicating with angels and spirit guides, mindfulness and meditation.

Everything I have experienced on my journey so far has prepared me for this work. My mission is to heal. My calling is to write and teach. My soul whispers to me to leave behind a meaningful legacy that will pave the way for others and help them find their own light.

My North Node is in Capricorn, placed in the sixth house. I am here to guide and serve.

Embracing my differences is a gift, and I intend to fulfil my life's mission by serving the universe.

With all my heart,

Yves

FOREWORD

I have been thinking about writing a book on tarot for many years. However, as I am self-taught, I was often daunted by the vast number of books that had already been written on the subject. Each method seemed different, and I wasn't sure where to begin. It felt as though each author had their own approach to reading the cards. This may be fine for professionals, but for beginners like me at the time, it's a different story entirely.

Firstly, I had to choose between the method passed down to me by my grandmother, the American method, and the French method. This was a daunting task, especially since the traditional card games — the Tarot of Marseille and the Rider-Waite Tarot — are quite different.

Over time, I set these aside and worked with the Tarot of Marseille for several years. The origin of this Tarot remains debated, but it has the unique quality of showing neutral yet expressive images, particularly in the Minor Arcana. However, this also presented a challenge. While the Tarot of Marseille is an exceptional tool for clairvoyance, the Minor Arcana are not beginner-friendly.

Therefore, I decided to start by focusing on the Major Arcana. But I was also drawn to the Rider-Waite deck. The challenge with the Rider-Waite deck is that it is highly illustrated and filled with scenes of all kinds.

On the other hand, it's much easier to read. Take the Three of Swords, for example: the difference between the two versions is striking.

However, I eventually realised that the Rider-Waite could be misleading. The reader is often limited by the scene shown on the card, which leaves little room for pure clairvoyance and prevents images, sounds, colours and feelings from emerging freely. For this reason, I re-explored the minor arcana of the Tarot of Marseille. These cards are simple and free of visual distractions, with strong links to numerology. These qualities offer undeniable advantages.

This book is the result of my personal experiences and moments of doubt. Very little has been written about the minor arcana in connection with the Tarot of Marseille. Yet these cards offer insights that are deeply related to our daily lives. Although connecting with higher spiritual truths is important for personal growth, we are still human beings living on Earth, facing its many challenges and uncertainties.

I hope that, with the help of this book and the growing interest in tarot, you will gain wisdom that is often difficult to grasp without losing sight of its spiritual essence. I invite you to approach it with an open heart and a sincere spirit, and to embrace lifelong transformation.

I also hope that it will inspire you to pass this knowledge on to others one day. Don't be daunted by the 78 cards, which may seem like relics from the Middle Ages. Instead, view them as steps that you can take, one by one, to free your soul from the patterns that are holding you back. Each one will bring you closer to breaking free from the habits that lead to repeated mistakes.

I sincerely hope that you will experience as much joy reading this book as I did writing it.

With all my love,
Yves

INTRODUCTION

The origins of the Tarot remain shrouded in mystery. Some claim that it was created by the ancient Egyptians or Babylonians, also known as the Chaldeans. Others claim that it originated in India or China. Some mention the Templars, while others believe that it was the gypsies who spread it across Europe. Regardless of its origin, this powerful tool continues to grow in popularity thanks to its simplicity, offering direct access to universal truth.

The Tarot is based on the idea that all truth, wisdom, and the answers to our questions already exist within us. Our soul already knows them. It is as though all divine knowledge is reflected in this oracle, providing us with a means of accessing that immense source of wisdom — if we have the key.

The Tarot is a guide that helps us to understand ourselves better. In many ways, it feels alive and is constantly evolving. It serves as both an exoteric tool for divination and an esoteric tool for self-knowledge. Furthermore, it is an endless source of life lessons — a true school of life.

The Tarot also has universal appeal because it gives life meaning and provides answers to existential questions. Through its teachings, we learn to relate better to others. We come to understand the crises, hardships, and empty spaces that punctuate our lives. Humanity is like a vast family: each of us is unique, yet we are all connected by shared experiences. If there is one goal we all have in common, it is to achieve unconditional love.

One of the most beautiful things about tarot is how accessible it is. Anyone can learn its language. However, pure intentions, free from ego, are required to see beyond surface-level interpretations. As the saying goes, 'Don't throw your pearls to swine.'

Above all, tarot is a guide. It mirrors the human soul, helping you to understand the rhythms and cycles that shape your life. It encourages you to make conscious choices and reminds you that life is a journey of discovery, not a predetermined path.

This book focuses on the Tarot of Marseille, consisting of 78 arcana divided into two categories. The 22 major arcana represent divine sparks or sacred symbols. The 56 minor arcana are split into two further groups: the numbers one to ten for each of the four suits — Wands, Cups, Pentacles, and Swords — and the court cards: Pages, Knights, Queens and Kings. Together, the minor arcana reflect the material (Earth), mental (Air), emotional (Water) and spiritual (Fire) planes.

I encourage you to make your Tarot deck a daily companion. The more you practise, the more familiar you will become with this intuitive art. If you are just starting out, try drawing a single card each day (you will find a sample reading at the end of the book). Gradually, you will learn the meanings of the cards and begin to notice how they guide you through daily life.

Keep a journal of your experiences. This logbook will serve as a personal record of your tarot journey, filled with your own insights and reflections, as well as the symbols that are most meaningful to you. Just as with dream symbols, certain cards will resonate with you in unique ways.

In writing this book, I don't claim to have reinvented tarot – far from it. My goal is simply to make this profound and complex art more accessible and help you grow with it. This book will guide you, step by step, towards discovering your true self. The journey will not be without its challenges. Tarot has a way of reflecting the hidden parts of ourselves. It's easy to misinterpret a reading, only to realise later that the tarot was right all along. Keep an open heart and be ready to receive the messages your soul is sending you. As the saying goes, 'Forewarned is forearmed.'

May this book fill you with wisdom. It is one of the greatest gifts you can give yourself.

GUIDELINES

- Remember: The cards you draw are not the result of chance; they contain an important message for you.

- When drawing a Major Arcana card, take the time to identify its distinctive features. After studying the card closely, you can then refer to the relevant section in the following pages:

- General Description: This section includes a brief description of the relevant arcana and will help you familiarise yourself with the card's symbolism.

- The Characters: This section refers to the people that the arcana can represent. This section sheds more light on the people around you. However, if your question concerns a situation rather than a specific person, you may not find the clues you need to interpret the arcana.

- The Personality: This section provides insight into the various aspects of the question. It lists the qualities and possible defects of the relevant arcana and describes their physical and emotional lives and general state of health. Depending on the question, this section may also refer to the consultant or any other relevant person.

- The Arcana Applied to Your Daily Life: This section provides answers to general questions. It offers various ways of interpreting events in the consultant's life. Due to its predictive nature, it can support clairvoyance. There are many possibilities with this section.

- Keywords to Complete the Interpretation: To help you understand the arcana better, we have added a few keywords for more information. This section often reflects the consultant's state of mind and presents important points to consider in order to apply the card's wisdom fully.

- How to integrate the vibration of the arcana: As you read this section, allow the words to permeate you and vibrate the strings of your soul. You will feel as if the message is going straight to your heart rather than your brain. Be receptive to this vibration that transcends time and space.

INTRODUCTION TO TAROT READING

Key 1: Dispelling Myths Surrounding the Tarot

There are no specific times that are more favourable than others for tarot readings. A consultation can occur at any time; there is no need to wait for a full moon, a particular day of the week or a specific date. Neither Sunday nor Friday the 13th has any special influence on a reading. Tarot can be practised at any time of the year, month, week or day.

Tarot reading is also a professional activity that deserves fair compensation. Becoming a tarot reader requires time, study and dedicated practice. Like any other profession, it requires effort and skill, and readers have bills to pay like everyone else. In an ideal world, it might be possible to share this knowledge freely, but even then, some people would still try to take advantage of your skills, time, and generosity. It is not wrong to ask for payment for your services. At the very least, a client should thank the reader at the end of a session. Gratitude is the least they can show.

Some tarot readers enjoy adding flair to their practice by wearing eccentric outfits or using props such as crystal balls. These choices are personal and do not reflect the true quality of a tarot reader. Skill cannot be measured by the size of one's library or collection of esoteric items.

Some readers spread fear by making dramatic predictions. However, most clients find such messages unhelpful. It is far more valuable and beneficial to explain why certain events occur and what lessons can be learned from them.

Key 2: What You Need for a Personal Draw or Consultation

First, you need a Tarot deck that resonates with you. There are hundreds of decks available, and it is up to you to choose the one that speaks to you the most. In this book, we recommend either the Tarot of Marseille or the Rider-Waite Tarot.

You will also need a small round table for consultations or a small altar. Cover this surface with a cloth in a soft, spiritual colour, or even a combination of colours. Good choices include white, mauve, purple, dark blue or gold. Your lighting should be gentle and subdued. Some readers prefer daylight, while others find a dimmer setting more suitable. Let your personal energy and sensitivity to light guide you. The consultation space should be tastefully decorated to foster a sense of trust. Ideally, all consultations should be performed in the same room.

As a tarot reader, you should dress appropriately and tastefully. If you wish to light a candle or burn incense, ensure that the candle is unscented and only burn the incense before or after the session. Some clients may have allergies, so it is better to avoid any potentially bothersome scents.

Turn off your phone and other electronic devices during a consultation. You may play soft background music to help block out external noise, but make sure it does not distract from your intuitive work.

If you practise tarot professionally, it is wise to have two decks: one for your clients and one for your personal use. Always purify your decks with incense after each reading.

Note: magnetise your deck and, most importantly, do not lend it to anyone. Keep it in a quiet place, wrapped in a cloth or in a case for protection.

Key 3: The Essential Qualities of a Tarot Reader

A tarot reader must be generous and have a genuine desire to serve others. Their role is to provide guidance and advice with respect and tact.

Being a tarot reader is a full-time commitment, whether practised professionally or not. Prioritise your health by eating well, getting enough sleep, exercising, meditating and seeking therapy if needed, to remain in the best possible state of mind. Avoid alcohol, drugs or any medication that may impair your mental clarity or judgement, including antidepressants, anxiolytics or narcotics — especially if you are unwell or exhausted.

It is important to remain calm. Never perform a reading for yourself or anyone else if you are stressed, overwhelmed or short on time.

Before drawing the cards, surround yourself with a protective, luminous aura. It is good practice to meditate, say a prayer and connect with your guides, guardian angels or God, according to your beliefs. This will help to prevent your ego from interfering with the reading.

Ground yourself like a tree. Stand with your feet firmly on the ground, stay aware of the present moment and reach for the sky. This connection with the earth and the universe will help you to stay centred and present. Take your time. There is no need to rush.

A tarot reading is a sacred act. Do not allow outsiders to attend your consultations or personal readings.

The Interpretation of the Tarot Arcanas

Interpreting tarot arcanas is not an easy task. This book provides a straightforward and effective approach to learning the basics. It includes a chapter on the Major Arcana, relating to different aspects of our lives, and another on the Minor Arcana, which will be covered in the second book and helps refine your interpretations. This section also presents various methods of laying out the cards, ranging from simple spreads to more complex ones.

Key 4: The Flow of a Consultation

When it comes to the flow of a consultation, choose the type of spread that suits you best. Hold the deck in your hands and centre yourself. Focus on one question at a time and phrase your questions positively. For instance, if you want information about a job opportunity, ask, 'Am I going to get this job?' rather than 'Am I going to be rejected again?'

Shuffle the cards for as long as you feel is necessary. If a card flies out or falls to the ground, it is no accident. It is a direct message from the Universe and a key part of the reading, so it should be included.

Cut the deck with your non-dominant hand, often called the 'hand of the heart'. You can also spread the cards face down in a fan-like motion. Begin with the question that concerns you the most. Draw the cards one by one and lay them out according to the chosen spread (you will find examples of these at the end of the book).

If you are not satisfied with the answer you receive, there is no need to ask the same question again. Repeating the question will not change the result. However, if you would like more information, you can draw a second card to shed more light on the reading.

Key 5: Interpreting the Chosen Cards

After drawing your cards, do not begin reading them right away. Take a moment to observe all the cards you have drawn. Allow images, sensations, impressions, discomforts or emotions to come to you. Avoid filtering your thoughts or making any judgements. Simply accept what comes naturally.

When you examine the cards, you may notice certain patterns or details. These can be important clues for interpreting the spread. Ask yourself if you notice any of the following:

- The absence or emphasis of the major/minor arcanas.
- The absence or accentuation of reversed cards.
- Predominance of one element, such as Earth or Fire.
- The absence or accentuation of court cards.
- Repetition of a specific number, such as several eights.
- Predominance of a tarot family.

All of these observations have meaning. This book, along with the second volume, will help you to understand and interpret them.

When you feel ready, analyse each card individually to uncover its message. Write your findings in a notebook to track your interpretations and progress. This habit is especially helpful for beginners. It enables you to reflect on past readings, observe how predictions have unfolded and grasp how the lessons have been incorporated into your life.

As you progress, your intuition and logbook will become more important than the theoretical meanings of the cards. Remember that each tarot card tells a unique story connected to the consultant's reality.

There is no set rule for how often you should draw cards. However, large spreads, such as annual or astrological readings, should only be done once a year. Sometimes, you may find that the tarot does not seem to speak to you. In those cases, it is better to use a different oracle or put your tarot cards aside for a few days.

Key 6: Reversed Cards

Reversed cards are a delicate subject, and interpretations vary widely. Many tarot readers choose to ignore their meanings altogether, reading the cards as if they were upright. Despite the variety of opinions, one thing is clear: beginners should first master the basics of tarot before exploring the added complexity of reversed cards. Although they offer valuable insights, reversed cards can also increase the risk of confusion.

In my experience, the biggest mistake when reading reversed cards is assuming that they always mean the opposite of their upright meaning. While this may sometimes be the case, reversed cards often point to something much deeper in the consultant's life.

Each tarot card represents a particular energy at work. This energy may be strong or weak, focused or scattered, or close or distant in time. When a card appears reversed, it often suggests that the energy is not manifesting properly, either partially or with difficulty.

Sometimes, you may draw one or more reversed cards. These can have various meanings, so here are some things to bear in mind when you encounter them:

- A reversed card may indicate that the situation is unclear. Certain missing elements may delay the outcome of the project, or perhaps something better will come along later.

- Consider whether the consultant feels stuck or believes they have taken the wrong path.

- The consultant may be hiding from their true self, perhaps by wearing a mask or creating a false identity.

- They may be resisting or blocking significant events that need to happen, often out of fear of rejection or the unknown. In this case, the reversed card highlights a part of their personality that they are not acknowledging.

- It may also reflect the consultant's refusal to experience an important life lesson. Sometimes, a reversed card signals a void in their life. From a psychological perspective, it may be wise to reflect on your projections, denials or overcompensations.

- Sometimes, a person must hit rock bottom before realising the need for change. A reversed card may serve as a warning sign.

- The consultant may be encouraged to take an unconventional path. In some cases, the reversed card suggests that they should swim against the current and move beyond their comfort zone.

Finally, you may wonder whether a consultant is doomed to suffer the fate suggested by a reversed card. The answer is no. A person warned by the Tarot is better prepared. It is their responsibility to make the necessary changes to their life. This begins with understanding who they truly are and making adjustments to the parts of their life that no longer serve them.

KEY 7

THE MAJOR ARCANAS

CHAPTER 1

THE MAGICIAN

The Magician archetype represents the beginning of everything. He knows how to bring ideas and intuitions to life. He is active and creative, moving forward by drawing on his strengths and seemingly limitless resources. This skilful and spontaneous figure also possesses great self-confidence, motivating him to repeatedly take on new projects.

However, the Magician can also be naive and impatient. His inexperience may lead him down questionable paths. He often becomes overwhelmed by his illusions, which can result in failure. The Magician must learn to recognise and control his urge to manipulate others, as well as his selfish and self-satisfied tendencies.

Characters

A child, a teenager, a student, a man, a husband, a lover, a brother, an artist, a person with a young mind, a curious and imaginative individual, a dreamer, a liar, a selfish opportunist, or someone who is pushy or manipulative.

Personality

Qualities:

- Likes to create, innovate and launch new projects, and thinks outside the box
- Ingenious, self-taught, resourceful and talented, jack-of-all-trades
- Pioneer
- Leader: an undisputed leader
- Intelligence above average
- Lively and spontaneous mind, constantly alert
- Daring, genius
- Makes things happen
- Moves society forward
- Great personal ambitions
- Short-term vision, takes advantage of the present
- Lover of life
- Communicative joy of living
- Ball of energy, can't stay still
- Radiant
- Proud
- Presence, confidence, and charisma
- Ease of speech
- Able to move, captivate, and persuade his listeners
- Desire for freedom and independence
- Hates wasting time
- Doesn't complicate life
- Success and recognition
- Thirst for knowledge

Faults:

- Ignores his talents and doubts his skills
- No self-control
- Impulsive

- Needs to be admired and is sensitive to flattery
- Black sheep
- Depressed
- Escalates problems
- Engages in scams and shady business
- Uses others for their own benefit
- Refuses to mature or take responsibility

- Liar
- Arrogant
- Boastful
- Unscrupulous
- Narcissistic
- Self-centered
- Provocative
- Superficial
- Head in the clouds, restless

Love life:

- In search of a soulmate
- Love is the heart of their existence
- Wants to please and seduce
- Likes renewal and fantasy
- Pleasant and friendly in relationships

- Proud and generous
- Picky about friends and lovers
- Holds appearance in high regard
- Needs solitude at times
- Hates routine
- Passionate

Reverse Card in Relation to Love:

- Afraid to lose individuality and freedom in relationships
- Frivolous

- Relationship structure is often dominant and dominated
- Afraid to commit

- Accumulates many short-lived adventures

- Plays with their partner's feelings and emotions

Professional Life:

- Self-taught and resourceful

- Great intellectual skills

- Uses their creativity and ingenuity

- Enjoys leading and being their own boss

- Takes initiative

- Manual skills

Reverse Card in Relation to Career:

- Dispersion and difficulty in concentrating their energy

- Inexperience

- Incompetence

- Lack of self-confidence

- Ignores their potential

- Immobility

- Addiction

- Contested

- Imposes his will and decisions

- Difficulty recognising mistakes

- Lack of initiative

Health:

- Weak points: heart, lungs, breathing, blood circulation, spine, eyes, face

- Nervousness and stress

- Migraines

- Skin problems

The Magician Applied to Your Daily Life

- A new project arises, such as a romantic relationship, a job, or a birth.

- Now is the time to harness your qualities and talents.

- Stop thinking and get started. Dare!

- Don't be afraid to take action.

- Be creative and innovative.

- Share your opinion and speak up.

- Learn to use your free will and get to the point.

- Simplify your life.

- Set yourself your life goals and take the necessary steps to achieve them.

- Breathe some magic into your life.

- See life through childish eyes and try to take yourself less seriously.

Keywords to Complete the Interpretation

- Creative and original
- Ingenious
- Versatile and flexible
- Great potential
- Gifts, innate talents

- Power of persuasion
- Adaptability
- Spontaneous
- Ambitious
- Sense of initiative

Reverse card:

- Selfishness
- Absence of scruples
- Doubts about potential, talents, and abilities
- Undecided
- Immature
- Difficulty picking themselves up after a failure
- Difficulty with self-control
- Jealous
- Authoritarian
- Superficial

How to Integrate the Vibration of the Magician

To do so, you must identify a project and see it through to completion. You cannot afford to doubt yourself or spread your focus too thinly. You need to focus your energy on a goal and turn your ideas into concrete action. Don't take anything for granted, even if you possess all the qualities necessary for success. Success must be earned!

CHAPTER 2

THE HIGH PRIESTESS

The High Priestess archetype represents the wisdom of the soul. She is defined by her unparalleled intuition and deductive abilities, coupled with intelligent thinking. The High Priestess is mysterious by nature and invites us to seek personal knowledge and self-discovery. She is governed by the cycles of the universe and represents the feminine aspect in every sense.

However, the High Priestess can become passive and allow life to pass her by. Influenced by hasty judgements, she sometimes fails to apply meaningful knowledge to her own life. She is deeply emotional and must be mindful of her sensitive nervous system and often shifting temperament. Her challenge is to face and reconcile this inner duality.

Characters

She can be a wife, a friend, a mistress, a mother, a mother-in-law, a sister-in-law, a sister, a grandmother, a lawyer, a judge, a detective, a nurse, a doctor, a psychologist or a midwife.

Personality

Qualities

- Comfortable in a healthy, calm, and harmonious atmosphere
- Possesses a kind, simple and patient soul
- Welcoming and hospitable
- A listening ear
- Discreet, reserved and serious
- Needs to retire to recharge
- Gets to the point and remains quiet if she has nothing to say
- Cautious and far-sighted, inclined to save others
- More dominated by emotion than by intellect
- Friendship is sacred to them
- Powerful charisma
- Ability to associate with others
- Called upon by human distress
- Strong taste for real or imaginary trips
- Fertile imagination and creative intelligence
- Interested in esoteric, metaphysical, and spiritual studies
- Mysterious and enigmatic
- Rich inner life, meditation, search for the meaning of life
- Hates confrontation and lies
- Phenomenal intuition
- Embodies sensitivity

Faults:

- Difficult to approach, distant, and hostile
- Closed to all communication
- Psychological state constantly in flux
- Lack of self-confidence

- Undecided, watches life go by
- Hypersensitive and lets herself be lulled by the rhythm of her emotions
- Difficulty making her wishes come true
- Hates taking orders or being rushed

- Tendency towards depression and paranoia
- Attracted by mediumship; wants to capture attention by focusing on mystery and secrecy
- Multiple personalities
- Cares too much for herself

Love Life:

- Embodies the ideal partner
- Love is a pure and lofty feeling
- Wise and full of compassion
- Love for life
- Warm, affectionate, loyal and devoted
- Great sensitivity

- Romantic and naive, with a big heart
- Spontaneous
- Joy of living
- Need for silence and solitude in love
- Relationship built day by day based on communication

Reverse Card in Relation to Love:

- Platonic love, with no warmth or sensuality
- No spontaneity of heart

- Reserved
- Excessively shy
- Unable to communicate
- Suppresses her feelings

- Secret love or extramarital affair
- Passive, waiting for their Prince Charming or a Princess
- Is afraid of fully merging with their partner
- Rejection, loneliness and boredom

- Unable to give
- Afraid of commitment
- In relationships, tries to gain an advantage
- Lack of openness

Professional Life:

- Talent for long term studies, analysis, and in-depth research
- Takes several years to find her calling
- Has to get to know herself better, especially with regard to her hidden qualities
- Updates her gifts and talents through work
- Reflects or work in a team

- Feels fulfilled through work
- Understands the depth of the human psyche
- Talented in guiding and advising
- Fascinated by the truth and by the hidden secrets of the world
- Can understand and empathise with others when they are distressed

Reverse Card in Relation to Career:

- Has difficulty making informed choices

- Lack of knowledge causes incompetence

- Her decisions are guided by false intuitions

- Has difficulty completing projects

- Lazy, immobile and lacking motivation

- Upstart syndrome

- Refuses to share professional knowledge

- Individualism

- Haughty attitude

- Can experience conflict with colleagues

Health:

- Must learn to control negative emotions

- Mood disorders (bipolar, cyclothymia and depression)

- Weakness of the reproductive system (ovaries, uterus, breasts, prostate, etc.)

- Latent diseases (tumors, cancers, hernias)

- Left eye and the entire left side of the body (reflects emotions)

- Neck area, mouth, larynx, thyroid, and throat

- Digestive system and stomach, abdominal region

The High Priestess Applied to Your Daily Life

— Follow your intuition.

— Take a step back from your question — now is not the time to make a decision.

— Some details are still unknown. Let events unfold naturally.

— A project or person is about to begin.

- A secret will be revealed to you.

- It is time to begin your spiritual journey.

- Immerse yourself in your inner self and try to understand the mistakes you have made in the past.

- Time is on your side. Meditate more on the matter!

- It's time to satisfy your curiosity: learn, study and undertake training.

- Pull back and take a holiday.

- Balance your emotions and try to take a broader view of life.

- Write down your dreams and aspirations. Their meaning will become clearer.

- Open up to the unknown.

- Highlight the parts of your personality that you have hidden for years.

- Stop fussing and stay calm.

Keywords to Complete the Interpretation

- Reserved, calm and wise

- Caring and welcoming

- Mature and serious

- Patient

- Goal-oriented

- Great sensitivity

- A listening ear

- Intuitive and receptive to feelings and senses

- Charismatic and naturally authoritative

- Observer
- Simple and straight to the point
- Loyal
- Imaginative

Reverse Card:

- Concealer and hypocrite
- Resentful
- Conservative and stubborn
- Intolerant
- Suspicious
- Distant, cold and indifferent
- Lazy
- Passive and amorphous
- Vulnerable
- Shy
- Finds it difficult to express herself and withdraws inwardly
- Lack of self-confidence
- Fear of getting involved
- Lack of generosity, frankness, and spontaneity
- Avoid compromising themselves

How to Integrate the Vibration of the High Priestess

In order to embrace the energy of the High Priestess, you must confront the dormant duality within yourself. Start by learning to calm your mind and control your emotions. In this state of deep serenity, you will encounter your true self at the core of your being. Once you have identified the various facets of this inner duality, a lesson will present itself. The High Priestess arcana invites you to be receptive to divine laws and to what comes from above.

THE EMPRESS

The Empress archetype represents the feminine qualities found in all of us, such as love, sensuality, nurturing, warmth, fertility and harmony. Her power stems from feelings, intuition, and the great cycles of nature. The Empress determines the motivation that drives a person to act. She governs all the pleasures of existence, particularly those of the heart.

However, the Empress can sometimes use her powers of seduction for questionable purposes. She may misjudge situations when blinded by emotions. Envy and frustration can prevent her from embracing abundance, leaving her unable to realise her full potential. In such moments, she may succumb to lust or excessive materialism.

Characters

She is a mother, a wife, a daughter, a sister, a lover, a writer, a teacher, an artist, a pregnant woman, an intelligent, cultivated, educated woman, a seductress and a haughty, proud, pretentious woman.

Personality

Qualities:

- Soft and warm
- Calm, thoughtful
- Welcoming, sociable
- Generous
- Charmer
- Hates vulgarity
- Physically active
- Likes to travel and get away from it all
- Nature lover
- Marvels at the simple things in life
- Savours the little joys of existence
- Very creative
- Ability to transmit knowledge
- Likes dress well and be elegant
- Attracts many friendships
- Cares about others for who they are, not what they do
- Does not like to be involved in arguments or complicate the life of others
- Communication is the engine of her existence
- Highly intellectual with strong brain activity
- Needs to understand and acquire new knowledge
- Great mental and intuitive strength
- A thousand projects in mind and the know-how to bring them to fruition
- Likes to party and be in good company

Faults:

- Arrogant and conceited
- Asocial and isolates himself
- Condescending, contemptuous and jealous
- Authoritarian
- Proud
- Sensitive to flattery
- Focused on appearances and extravagant tastes
- Impatient
- Overestimates
- Interested in success, afraid of failure
- Refuses to grow up
- Scattered, frivolous and lost in life, unable to carry out projects
- Resigns from life
- Critical

Love Life:

- Warm and affectionate with loved ones
- Takes good care of their people
- Gives without keeping score
- Romantic, caring and spiritual
- Always in a good mood
- Likes to have many friends
- Has a deep and lasting love
- A life without love is not worth living
- An open book

Reverse Card in Relation to Love:

- Volatile and unstable
- Accumulates conquests
- Rather lie to cover themselves than admit defeat

- Intense need to be loved
- Desires popularity
- Superficial
- Wishes to be in the spotlight
- Master of the art of seduction
- Hates being alone

- Sensitive to rejection
- Seeks the satisfy personal needs
- Confuses love and friendship
- Low self-esteem

Professional Life:

- Above-average intelligence
- Multi-talented
- Creative
- Versatile
- Must choose a path that really speaks to them to stay motivated

- Gift of passing on knowledge
- Thirst for learning
- Has the ability to express herself
- Ability to accomplish multiple tasks

Reverse Card in Relation to Career:

- Overestimates their skills
- Learned rigidity
- Locks herself in a form of security out of fear of the unknown
- Refusal to work in a team

- The end justifies the means
- Time is money, and everything comes at a price!
- Interested meetings with the ultimate goal of advancing one's career

- Lack of imagination, only mechanically repeating what has been learnt
- Lack of lucidity
- Unrealistic expectations

- Refusal to adhere to a fixed schedule
- Full of herself
- Work overload

Health:

- Frantic pace of life
- Stress, anxiety and depression
- Weak points: head, brain, liver, intestines, blood pressure, prostate
- Weak immune system

- Reproductive system (infertility and genetic diseases)
- Must listen to the warnings from their body

The Empress Applied to Your Daily Life

- You meet love.

- It's time to express your affection. Allow yourself to be loved and pampered.

- Breathe a little more romance into your life.

- Reconnect with nature. Go outside and soak up the warm sunshine or tend to your garden.

- You give birth to a child, a project, or an idea.

- You are happy working with children or taking care of your own.

    – Treat yourself to the luxury of a massage or spa treatment.

    – Learn to receive and to please yourself.

    – You will be rewarded for your talents.

    – Feed your artistic passions: music, song, dance, painting, and theatre. Simply create!

    – You are going on a trip to broaden your horizons.

Keywords to Complete the Interpretation

- Powerful
- Creative
- Ability to communicate and teach
- Charming and elegant
- Sensual
- Dynamic
- Determined to carry out her projects
- Financial wealth
- Open-minded
- Patient
- Friendly
- Joy of living
- Logical and thoughtful with a great capacity for discernment
- Practical spirit
- Needs to understand and know

Reverse Card:

- Authority
- Critical
- Conventional
- Importance of appearance
- Too cerebral; ignores the impulses of their body

- Proud, condescending and contemptuous

- Capricious

- Frivolous

- In the grips of lust

- Scattered, does several things at once

- Refuses to grow up

- Difficulty concentrating

- Thinks too much

How to Integrate the Vibration of the Empress

Empress, you must nurture the projects that truly matter to you. First, however, you need to practise the discipline required to free yourself from less meaningful obligations. The risk lies in becoming trapped in your imagination or retreating into empty, theoretical ideas. The Empress's vibration requires genuine commitment, whatever your passions may be. Above all, do not cling to the past or seek love outside yourself. Love from others can easily become a distraction. Everything you need is already within you.

CHAPTER 4

THE EMPEROR

The Emperor archetype embodies masculine qualities such as authority, power, leadership, ambition and rationality. With a strong sense of organisation and realisation, the Emperor is anchored in the power of materialisation. He also embodies self-control, common sense, and respect for rules.

However, the Emperor can be stubborn and inflexible in his thinking. Attracted by profit, he often relies on rigid logic that leaves little room for emotion. His fear of the unknown and of change can cause him to adopt a defensive attitude, slowing his personal growth.

Characters

He is a man, a parent, a father, a husband, a stepfather, a boss, a businessman, an adversary and a determined, influential and authoritarian figure who is rigid, domineering and devoid of emotion.

Personality

Qualities:

- Frank and honest
- Responsible
- Disciplined
- Meticulous
- Very determined
- Discreet and peaceful
- Patient
- Careful in all aspects
- Symbol of strength and perseverance
- Driven by exceptional strength
- Craftsman of his own life
- Has a spirit of analysis, logic, and synthesis
- Studies a situation from all angles before taking action
- Sense of repartition
- Outstanding organiser
- Workaholic
- Aware of his own worth and abilities
- Knows how to grow his assets

Faults:

- Anguish
- Unstable and malleable character
- Stubborn and refuses to change
- Doesn't like to be contradicted or interrupted
- Petty and tactless
- Doesn't appreciate what he has
- Angry, has difficulty controlling his emotions
- Authoritarian, tyrannical, imposes his will on others
- Very marked feeling of inferiority
- Suffers from chronic insecurity

- Uncompromising; nothing and nobody lives up to his expectations
- Proud, thinks everything is because of him
- Too serious
- Lacks initiative
- Appearance-oriented and always comparing himself to others

- Stingy and materialistic; defined by money
- Takes advantage of the people around him
- Unable to support himself
- Seeks prestige and glory
- Routine
- Susceptible

Love Life:

- Loyal
- Sincere
- Reserved
- Seeks emotional stability and security
- Careful in love

- Marriage takes time, thought, and preparation; doesn't rush into it
- Meets a romantic partner in his thirties
- Homosexuality

Reverse Card in Relation to Love:

- Cold, does not show any emotion
- Timid
- Possessive

- Undemonstrative
- Dreads involvement with another and is afraid of losing control

- Self-centered
- Domineering
- Stubborn
- Not very empathetic or attentive to his partner's needs
- Love feels like a sign of weakness

- Complicated relationship
- Relationship based on money and power imbalance
- Fears his partner
- Purely sexual relationship
- Inflexible

Professional Life:

- Disciplined
- Meticulous and rigorous
- Discreet
- Responsible
- Devoted
- Great concentration
- Leadership skills
- Ability to grow his income

- Ability to make thoughtful decisions
- Can bring projects to fruition
- Ability to plan and organise
- Need for security and stability
- Work is at the heart of his existence
- Analytical mind

Reverse Card in Relation to Career:

- Has difficulty delegating tasks
- Has difficulty working in a team
- Demonstrates ill will

- Dictatorship
- Abuses his power
- Is overworked
- Lack of creativity

- Won't consider the ideas of others
- Restricted to excessive productivity

Health:

- Stress
- Hypercholesterolemia
- Hypertension
- Weakness of the cardiovascular system
- Stomach ulcers
- Overweight
- Alcoholism (liver and gallbladder issues)
- Carnal obsessions

The Emperor Applied to Your Daily Life

- It's time to assert your authority.

- You will have to make some important decisions. Weigh up the pros and cons and get started!

- You have to reorient your life. The time for change has come!

- Stop being manipulated and take back control of your life!

- Stop wasting your time — effort, concentration, and discipline are essential!

- Now is the time to give your life direction. Establish a career plan for the short, medium, and long term.

- Professionally, you are accountable to your boss.

- Your family needs you. Take all necessary steps to ensure their comfort and safety.

- You may want to start a family.

- Your talents are recognised. You get a promotion.

- Invest and secure your future. Plan ahead!

- Set aside your pride and learn from your mistakes so that you can grow wiser.

- Stop taking yourself so seriously! Add some whimsy to your life!

Keywords to Complete the Interpretation

- Persevering and determined
- Stable
- Mature
- Responsible
- Hardworking and disciplined
- Respects the law
- Confident in their abilities
- Analytical
- Dynamic and able to bring ideas to life
- Righteous and protective of the weak

Reverse Card:

- Inflexible and stubborn
- Authoritarian
- Foolish pride
- Susceptible
- Uncompromising
- Angry and violent
- Difficulty controlling emotions
- Lack of fantasy and humor
- Doesn't learn from his mistakes
- Tied to money

How to Integrate the Vibration of the Emperor

In order to do so, you must learn to harness the power of your inner masculine energy. It is essential to set limits for yourself and acquire wisdom within those boundaries. You also need to manage your tendency to dominate others. Remember that one person's freedom ends where another's begins.

Your greatest life lesson is learning to respect yourself and those around you. There will be times when you must control your anger and ambition, and honour both the law and individual freedoms. When you can laugh at yourself and stop taking things so seriously, you will have made significant progress. From then on, others will see you as a wise person who offers advice with patience, understanding and experience.

CHAPTER 5

THE POPE

The Pope archetype represents values and moral codes. Acting as a mediator, he balances spirituality and materialism in our daily lives. He embodies self-control and inner strength, among other qualities. The Pope seeks answers to the great metaphysical questions of existence.

However, he can sometimes show signs of fanaticism and dogmatism in his speech and behaviour. This can cause him to become blinded by his beliefs and lose touch with reality. Consequently, he may adopt questionable principles and develop a narrow point of view. This limited perspective can create a false sense of wisdom, resulting in misleading or meaningless advice.

Characters

A man in his fifties, a teacher, an educator, a tutor, a metaphysician, a guide, a priest, a counsellor, a philosopher, a doctor, a surgeon, a psychologist, a psychiatrist, a judge, a wise or influential person, a man of faith, a moraliser.

Personality

Qualities:

- Humble and forgiving
- Quiet and reserved
- Shy and easily worried
- Demonstrates wisdom and exceptional maturity
- Spontaneous
- Imbued with compassion and humanism
- Generous
- Spiritual
- Detached from material goods
- Great inner strength
- Adapts to any circumstance
- Savour the present moment
- Fascinated by the mysteries surrounding humanity
- Need to surpass oneself to support a cause
- Need to feel useful and help others
- Likes to advise and guide others
- Ease of transmitting knowledge
- Endowed with a sharp mind and a natural curiosity
- Great ease of speech
- Ambitious
- Exceeds own limits
- Goes headfirst into life and wants to take on challenges
- Strong interest in change, freedom, and escape
- Thirsty for knowledge
- Intuitive

Faults:

- Arrogant
- Social climber
- Immature in heart and mind
- Bitter towards life

- Self-centered
- Solitary
- Jealous and envious
- Resentful
- Very critical
- Nervous and irritable
- Liar and dishonest
- Closed off to any dialogue
- Moralising, radical, and categorical
- Need to be adulated, admired
- Master in the art of exploiting vulnerable people
- Judges himself very harsh
- Imposes an iron discipline
- Difficulty receiving orders
- Is defined by his diplomas
- Looks for solutions externally rather than questioning himself
- Refuses to see himself as he is
- Blinded by his passionate states
- Rigid in his beliefs

Love Life:

- Sacred union
- Relationship characterised by peace and serenity
- Happy in love
- Aspire to a nice and smooth married life
- Gentle, generous, and protective
- Committed and responsible
- Loyal
- Great need for freedom
- Impossible to put in a cage
- Attracts people who need to be brooded over

Reverse Card in Relation to Love:

- Complicated, jealous, and inconstant
- Emotionally dependent
- Impulsive and emotionally empty
- Self-centered
- Bitter and resentful
- Lack of judgement
- Liar and hypocrite
- Arguing for nothing in romantic and platonic relationships
- Chronic dissatisfaction
- Difficulty developing on a sentimental level
- Difficulty making real friends
- Refuses to fully commit
- Fear of long-term relationships
- Wishes to be free, like air
- Lives many adventures and through many divorces
- Unhappiness

Professional Life:

- Great intellectual qualities
- Rigorous
- Ability to analyze and solve problems
- Attracted by professions that highlight the qualities of the heart
- Creative in all areas
- Integrates religion, soul and spirituality in the performance of his duties
- Endowed with a wealth of knowledge based on his life experience
- Logical mind
- Passionate about his work

Reverse Card in Relation to Career:

- Difficulty entering into a dialogue with peers
- Imposes his ideas on others and being inflexible
- Lead with an iron fist
- Refuse to compromise
- Wants to control everything
- Abuse of authority and plays power games
- Likes to receive honours and to be recognised
- Recognition based on reputation rather than expertise
- Susceptible
- Doubts the skills of others
- Megalomaniac

Health:

- Minor problems associated with old age, such as menopause or andropause, bone and joint fragility, difficulty moving, rheumatism, and arthritis
- Arrhythmia
- Infertility or difficulty in procreating
- Fibromyalgia
- Physical and mental hypertension
- Chronic diseases
- Sensitive nervous system
- Neurosis
- Depression and sickness
- Chronic fatigue
- Fainting

The Pope Applied to Your Daily Life

- It's high time you started playing by the rules.

- Be less superficial and deepen your knowledge.

- Life asks you to answer the following big questions: 'Who are you?' and 'What is your life's purpose?'

- You question your faith and your core values.

- Join a group or organisation that shares your ideals.

- Find the sacred centre at the heart of your being by meditating, praying and finding silence within yourself.

- Undertake an initiatory journey to encourage self-reflection and spiritual growth.

- Become aware of your core values and determine whether they remain relevant.

- Change what is preventing you from moving forward.

- Ask yourself what place God has in your daily life.

- Stop bringing everything back to yourself and learn to serve others.

- Listen to your inner voice and be mindful of the judgements you make about others.

- Guilt no longer has a place in your life. What dreams have you stifled all these years? It's time to make them happen!

- Let yourself be guided by faith, not by what others will say.

- Silence the conditioning that inhabits you. Life is a school where you learn from your mistakes. Perfection does not exist.

- Listen to others with an open mind and don't impose your way of thinking on them.

Keywords to Complete the Interpretation

- Selfless
- Empathetic and forgiving
- Good listening skills
- Conciliatory
- Serene
- Modest
- Patient
- Generous
- Honest
- Faithful
- Ability to question himself

- Competent
- Reliable
- Rigorous spirit
- Ability to solve problems
- Respected authority, but also feared
- Good advice
- Protective and reassuring
- Reasonable and wise
- Sense of duty

Reverse Card:

- Narrow-minded
- Categorical and radical
- Severe
- Criticism
- Moraliser
- Demanding
- Arrogant
- Fanatic
- Very conservative

- Intolerant
- Susceptible
- Influenced and vulnerable
- Desire to be admired
- Lack of experience
- Laxity
- Takes advantage of other's weaknesses to show off
- Resentful

How to Integrate the Vibration of the Pope

To do so, you must release all the conditioning that dictates your behaviour and rules of conduct. Once you have revealed your true self, you will begin to connect with your inner strength and deepest convictions. You will no longer feel the need to echo the words of others. Instead, you will speak and act from a place of authenticity.

The most significant lesson is to let go of the guilt, insecurities, and fears that prevent you from reaching your full potential. Now is the time to take back control of your life and confront the real or imagined demons that continue to haunt you. When you dare to look deep inside yourself, you will gain the respect and empathy of others. You will then be able to offer guidance and wisdom to those who seek your counsel.

CHAPTER 6

THE LOVER

The Lover archetype represents the choices we must make in life. There are always several possibilities available to us, and in order to evolve, it is essential to choose the best path. The Lover represents the harmonisation and integration of opposites, as in a couple where different values and perspectives converge. This archetype also reflects self-love and love for others, paying attention to appearances, forgiveness, and recognising our own vulnerability. It encourages us to engage fully in relationships while also being mindful of our inner world, balancing desire with wisdom and passion with understanding.

The Lover archetype often represents self-doubt, too. It highlights the difficulty of reconciling opposites, as well as the pitfalls of superficiality, such as false self-perception and the lies we tell ourselves. Consequently, there is a constant opposition between our true self and the self we aspire to become. This creates an ongoing conflict between our desires, beliefs, male and female polarities, reason and intuition. Recognising this tension is essential for personal growth because it invites introspection and honest reflection on the choices that shape our lives.

Characters

A couple, a teenager, a life partner, a seducer, an artist, a polyglot, an indecisive person, an actor, and a lover.

Personality

Qualities:

- Pleasant
- Sociable and likes human contact
- Warm
- Generous with his person and his time
- Good listening skills
- Sensitive and emotional
- Sentimental, romantic and dreamy
- Joy of living
- Spontaneous
- Creative
- Resourceful
- Clever
- Great adaptability
- Born communicator
- Has a natural charm
- Hungry for knowledge
- Intuitive
- Gives great importance to family and friends
- Seeks to please
- Has kept his childish side
- Can be rocked in the wind without worrying about tomorrow
- Embarked on all kinds of adventures
- Lives his life deeply and intensely

Faults:

- Anxious
- Superficial
- Lazy
- Naïve and very easily influenced
- Immature
- Irresponsible
- Manipulative; a master of evasion and seduction
- Lack of initiative
- Constantly doubting himself
- Wishes to look good in the eyes of others
- Eternally dissatisfied
- Dependent on others
- Seeks to capture attention
- Shamelessly steals other people's ideas
- Difficulty making decisions
- Disperses his energy and wants to do everything
- Ignores who he really is
- Refuses to question himself
- Fear of tomorrow and of responsibilities
- Fear of loneliness
- Unable to listen

Love Life:

- Love is the engine of his existence
- Gives pride of place to feelings and emotions
- Finds the right balance between emotional dependence and personal well-being
- Seeks harmony and sentimental happiness
- Endowed with a powerful magnetism
- Friendly and caring
- Eager for tenderness
- Falls in love easily
- In search of a soulmate
- Nothing fills him
- Gives without keeping score

Reverse Card in Relation to Love:

- Jealous and possessive
- Unfaithful and libertine
- Sees his partner as an object
- Avoids going out alone
- His passions are insatiable
- A series of short-lived romances to fulfill a deep need for love and attention
- Proud

Professional Life:

- Versatile
- Conscientious
- Meticulous
- Obedient
- Sense of organisation
- Keen intelligence
- Eternal student
- On the lookout for technological progress
- Seeks novelty
- Great adaptability
- Can accomplish several tasks at the same time
- Makes spontaneous decisions
- Likes human contact
- Promotes conciliation, discussion, and teamwork
- Feels the need to get to the bottom of things

Reverse Card in Relation to Career:

- Irresponsible
- Easily overwhelmed by events
- Doubts his abilities
- Lack of ambition; tendency to take the easy way out
- Plays chameleon to please everyone

- Lies in order to gain a promotion

- Inconsistency between ideas and actions

- Has difficulty combining work and personal life

- Shuns responsibility

- Chronic dissatisfaction and always being tempted to look elsewhere

- Bad career choices

Health:

- Very sensitive to stress

- Lack of vitality

- Constantly pushing physical limits

- Susceptible to lung diseases (asthma, bronchitis, and pneumonia)

- Learning disabilities

- Speech disorder

- Has periods of intense activity interspersed with involuntary rest periods

- Shallow breathing

The Lover Applied to Your Daily Life

- You are going to meet someone or start a relationship.

- Stop being cold and distant with others. Instead, learn to make friends with them.

- Show your love on a daily basis in all areas. Love! Love! Love!

- Do not resist — let yourself be seduced!

- Let yourself be guided by your desires and passions.

- Make love to let go of your feelings of inferiority and sexual guilt.

—   Identify your intentions and your position on a subject. You can then make an informed choice.

—   Stop doubting yourself and procrastinating. Trust life.

—   You are a victim of your own narrow-mindedness, which prevents you from seeing the bigger picture.

—   Create more harmony in your life by ceasing to compare yourself to others.

—   Take off your mask and stop trying to please others at all costs. Because, by doing so, you are only fuelling your chronic inattention.

—   What are your priorities in life? List them and work through them one by one.

—   You have nothing more to prove, but everything to be.

—   Simplify your life to love yourself better. Travel light and free yourself from your insecurities.

—   You are at a crossroads and must make important decisions. Stop burying your head in the sand!

Keywords to Complete the Interpretation

- Sensitive
- Curious
- Determined
- Discreet
- Enthusiastic
- Optimistic
- Young at heart
- Subtle
- Voluble
- Good communicator
- Likes to exchange and discuss

- Sentimental
- Friendly
- Good
- Sincere

- Good analytical skills
- Great adaptability
- Artistic sense
- Loves beautiful things

Reverse Card:

- Superficial
- Egocentric
- Profiteer
- Ambivalent and undecided
- Influenceable
- Inconstant
- Lack of self-confidence
- Skeptical
- Weakened by his sensitivity

- Passive and lazy
- Criticism
- Esthete
- Practices the cult of beauty
- Seducer
- Scatters their energies
- Eternal adolescent
- Arguing over nothing
- Weak in character

How to Integrate the Vibration of the Lover

Transparency is essential to integrate the vibration of the Lover. When you wear masks and project outward appearances, you lose touch with the deep roots of your identity. You may expend a lot of energy trying to please others and neglecting your own life, which goes against the natural laws of evolution. Understand that no one can provide the love you lacked in childhood. Take a step back, reflect, and release the doubts that cloud your mind. Use your creativity and natural enthusiasm for life to create meaningful work and avoid cycles of repeated disillusionment. Remember that life is not an endless carousel, but a spiral that rises towards wisdom and understanding — each choice offering the opportunity for growth.

CHAPTER 7

THE CHARIOT

The Chariot archetype inspires us to achieve our life goals. It provides the strength, focus and determination necessary for success. However, to reach these goals, we must first explore ourselves and uncover hidden qualities. This inner journey strikes a balance between the past and the future, and between the need for change and the desire for security. Everyone is the master of their own life, and mastery begins with understanding one's internal strengths and weaknesses. Only by exploring ourselves can we find true direction and purpose.

The Chariot can also signify an abuse of power, egocentricity and excess. It often reflects a lack of self-control and direction. When one seeks to control others due to a lack of self-awareness, rash acts may follow, driven by impulse. Life then becomes like a boat without a sail or rudder: adrift, lacking motivation, vision, long-term plans and goals. Recognising these tendencies enables one to regain balance and avoid becoming trapped by the illusions of control and authority over others.

Characters

A determined person, a person with a goal to achieve or a mission to accomplish, a director, an activist, a trainer, an educator, a diplomat, a public figure, a traveller, and an independent, intelligent, and creative person.

Personality

Qualities:

- Charitable and selfless soul
- Adorable
- Modest
- Conciliator
- Diplomatic
- Born leader
- Great sage
- Fine psychologist
- Determined
- Persevering
- Driven by unparalleled willpower
- Great self-confidence
- Idealist and progressive
- Creative and original
- Independent
- Unpredictable
- Avoids superficial relationships
- Observer
- Contemplative and meditative
- Insatiable curiosity
- Ease of learning
- Hates taking orders
- Doesn't complicate life
- Dislikes being the center of attention
- Likes to venture off the beaten track
- Likes to travel and broaden his horizons
- Attracted by change
- Remarkable intuition and prophetic gift
- Fascinated by the inexplicable
- Very intense inner life

- Needs solitude
- Great analytical skills
- Abhors conflict and gossip

- Gives his life a concrete purpose
- Patient

Faults:

- Self-centered
- Presumptuous
- Proud
- Power hungry
- Anguish
- Melancholy
- Paranoid
- Vanity
- Constant need for reassurance
- Compares himself to others
- Turns to artificial havens (alcohol, drugs, and medicine)
- Cannot distinguish the necessary from the superfluous
- Nervous

- Seeks prestige and gratification
- Flaunts his knowledge
- Extremely anxious
- Doesn't like to be controlled or directed
- Shuns responsibilities
- Chronic impulsivity
- Has no limits
- Never deprives himself of anything
- Stubborn
- Impatient
- Arrogant
- Hyperactive

Love Life:

- Demonstrative
- Passionate
- Frank
- Knows how to keep the flame alive
- Shines with a communicative joy for life
- Deep and lasting love
- Thrilling romantic relationship
- Sees love as a great friendship
- Has a great respect for his loved ones
- Wishes to protect his independence and his need for solitude
- Often prefers cohabitation to marriage
- Loves travelling as a couple

Reverse Card in Relation to Love:

- Cold
- Narcissistic
- Obstinate
- Difficulty making compromises
- Lack of respect for others
- Envious of the happiness of others
- Bitter towards life
- Fear of feeling imprisoned and losing his independence
- Numerous disagreements and personality conflicts
- Wants to rule everything
- Runs away from love
- Marriage usually ends in divorce
- Blocks his emotions

Professional Life:

- Ambitious and determined
- Ahead of their time
- Creative spirit
- Endowed with many talents and skills
- Great ease of learning
- Likes to travel
- Need to take on challenges
- Seeks to surpass themselves
- Comfortable in managerial or responsible positions
- Achieves the goals he sets for himself
- Knows success and achievement

Reverse Card in Relation to Career:

- Needs to feel superior to others
- Overconfidence
- Tactlessness
- Authoritarian
- Abuses his power and influence
- Upstart, opportunist
- Workaholic
- Goes beyond his limits
- Fear of moving forward and making necessary decisions
- Difficulty working in a team
- Difficulty making compromises
- Constantly wishing to change position
- Sudden departure without explanation
- Inordinate, unrealistic ambitions
- Only success matters
- Professional scandal

Health:

- Enjoys very good health
- Likes to be physically active
- Remains active throughout life
- Predisposed to cardiovascular arrest
- Constant need to move

- Victim of being overwork
- Subject to road accidents
- Feels depressed if tunable to get away and/or some fresh air

The Chariot Applied to Your Daily Life

- There's no point trying to control everything. Now is the time to take risks.

- Take back control of your life, even if it means changing direction.

- Stop dissipating your energy and focus on your goal.

- You will receive imminent news.

- Free yourself from your illusory sense of security and explore new horizons (e.g. travel, moving house, relocation).

- Hear the call of your soul. The time has come to fulfil your life's purpose.

- The efforts you have made to date will be rewarded.

- It's impossible to do everything in life. Clearly define your priorities and take the necessary steps to achieve them.

- Become aware of the feeling of failure within you. Change your attitude — desire is power!

- No matter what business you are in, it will be successful.

- If you feel that your life is stagnating and nothing motivates you anymore, take a fresh look at the areas you have neglected. See beyond your own limits.

- We're testing you. Learn to highlight your qualities as a leader and entrepreneur.

- Fight for the causes that matter to you. You were born to inspire, motivate and influence future generations.

- Do not stand in the way of change. Embrace it instead! It will be the start of a great adventure!

Keywords to Complete the Interpretation

- Selfless
- Charitable
- Creative
- Passionate
- Dynamic
- Courageous
- Determined
- Persevering
- Autonomous
- Responsible
- Conciliator
- Born leader
- Civilised
- Great self-control
- Self-confidence
- Needs to move
- Doesn't fear obstacles
- Wants to progress, advance, and succeed based on his own merits

- Completed
- Diplomat

- Aware of his individual and social responsibility

Reverse Card:

- Arrogant
- Proud
- Self-centered
- Narcissistic
- Nervous
- Anxious
- Stress
- Tyrannical
- Social climber
- Wants to understand and demonstrate everything
- Hyperactive
- Victim of the madness of grandeur

- Inconsistent
- Undecided
- Contradictory spirit
- Closed mind
- Gives up in the face of adversity
- Wants to triumph at all costs
- Victim of the madness of grandeur
- Needs space and freedom
- Tendency to isolate himself
- Shuns responsibilities
- Impulsive
- Aggressive and violent

How to Integrate the Vibration of the Chariot

To do so, you must embark on a journey of self-discovery. This arcana invites you to reflect on what is preventing you from moving forward. Self-analysis helps you to avoid rushing headfirst into events or forcing outcomes. The true challenge of the Chariot is to master the ego, including identity, emotions, impulses, desires, anger, power and control. Developing self-discipline enables you to understand where you are coming from and where you are going. Once this inner journey begins, peace of heart and mind may be achieved. Only then can the Chariot triumph over fate, because the shortest path in evolution is not always a straight line. There are always other avenues and choices to explore, and this journey enables you to navigate life with insight and wisdom.

CHAPTER 8

THE JUSTICE

The archetype of Justice embodies order and fairness. It embodies balance, especially when it comes to weighing up the pros and cons of situations. Justice encourages us to take responsibility for our actions, correcting mistakes in order to avoid repeating them. Although it may appear cold or overly analytical, this arcana is profoundly evolutionary. Indeed, it encourages wisdom by reminding us that we are all the authors of our own reality. We are what we create, and this is the law of cause and effect, or karma.

However, Justice can also reflect dishonesty, particularly in relation to legal matters or finances. In such cases, moral values may be cast aside and the end may be seen to justify the means. This lack of integrity may manifest as harshness of character, a sense of injustice or persecution. A person may attempt to impose their personal rules on others or blame misfortunes on heaven. Such behaviour causes the soul to regress, as unresolved elements of the past continue to reverberate into the present. Recognising these patterns enables us to restore fairness and integrity to our thoughts and actions.

Characters

A lawyer, a civil servant, a manager, a government administrator, someone from the Ministry of Revenue, a judge, an organiser, an administrator, someone who is righteous and just, an accountant, a police officer and someone who is divorced.

Personality

Qualities:

- Integrity and honesty
- Frank
- Loyal
- Generous
- Conservative
- Seeks stability
- Reasonable
- Curious by nature
- Great self-control; doesn't allow himself to relax
- Perfectionist
- Disciplined
- Very organised
- Ambitious
- Born leader
- Relentless logic
- Defends the causes close to his heart
- Needs to take action
- Sense of duty
- Able to take on responsibilities
- Likes the rules to be well established
- Obedient, follows laws and codes of conduct to a 'T'
- Respects the hierarchy
- Does not seek out attention or fame
- Always gives his all
- A fierce wrestler who rarely admits defeat
- Keen intelligence

Faults:

- Cold and not very empathetic
- Great dryness of heart
- Asocial
- Easily unbalanced
- Lazy
- Lack of initiative
- Very critical and offensive
- Biting repartee
- Aggressive and violent
- Cowardly
- Uncompromising with himself and others
- Proud
- Strong spirit of contradiction
- Stubborn and inflexible
- Impulsive
- Greedy for power and money
- Wants to dominate
- Feeling of insecurity
- In search of social elevation
- Opportunistic, profiteer
- Focused on satisfying one's own pleasures
- Outraged and refuse to comply with the established rules
- Compares himself to others
- Appearance matters to him
- Paranoid
- In the grip of an outburst of anger
- Inhabited by rage, a feeling of injustice
- Greatly misunderstood
- Complex and tormented
- Routine life
- Refuses to question oneself
- Fear of death and emptiness

Love Life:

- The head dominates the heart's impulses
- Honest and frank
- Places great importance on communication
- Needs to trust their partner and feel trusted in return
- Stability
- Deep feelings
- Betrayal is the ultimate insult
- Sharing
- Fills their partner with affection and attention of all kinds
- Marriage is an ideal to be achieved
- Seeks fantasy in marriage and engagement
- Inner peace

Reverse Card in Relation to Love:

- Relegating heart and feelings to the background
- Low self-esteem
- Immature at heart
- Jealousy
- Unfaithful
- Asocial
- Depressed when alone
- Does not open one's heart easily
- Love is a duty
- Lack of spontaneity and fantasy
- Constant need to receive proof of love
- Intolerant of one's partner
- Tensions and quarrels erupt very early in relationships
- Overwhelms their partner with reproaches
- Rupture and passionate drama
- Very difficult character

Professional Life:

- Tireless worker
- Disciplined
- Perfectionist
- Very organised
- Punctual
- Respects deadlines
- Competitive
- Versatile
- Great sense of synthesis
- Sense of command
- Ease of managing budgets and risks
- Has a long-term vision
- Administrator qualities
- Likes action and concrete achievements
- Needs to demonstrate his skills
- Takes some pride in the job title
- Leader temperament

Reverse Card in Relation to Career:

- Difficulty receiving orders
- Error in judgement and lack of objectivity
- Incapable of making decisions or taking sides
- Follows the rules to the letter, abandons their human side
- Moral codes are much too strict
- Bathed in shady affair
- Fear of not being successful in life
- Puts their own needs before those of others
- Constantly reproaches colleagues or his employees
- Hardness of character, inflexibility
- Uncompromising and intolerant of new ideas and the opinions of others
- Outrageous perfectionist

Health:

- Full of vitality
- Easily resists any form of disease
- Importance of eating well and exercising
- Fragility of the nervous system due to overwork
- Chronic fatigue

- Chronic migraines, neuralgia, and brain tumors caused by stress
- Weak kidneys, adrenal glands, heart, and female genitalia
- Serotonin disruption, which affects sleep
- Must listen to his body

The Justice Applied to Your Daily Life

- You are involved in various legal matters, including contracts, court cases, jury service, notarial deeds, property purchases and sales, inheritance, and marriage and divorce.

- Now is the time to regain balance. You are overworked and neglecting other areas of your life.

- You have to make an important decision. You have considered the pros and cons of the situation thoroughly. It's time to make a decision!

- Your core values are being challenged. Continue to build on your moral integrity — now is not the time to compromise. Do what's right.

- Take responsibility and keep your budget up to date. Do your accounting and pay your debts.

- A scenario you hadn't considered is emerging. Gather your courage and embrace the new path that lies ahead.

- Stop feeling sorry for yourself and accept the consequences of your actions. You are responsible for your own misfortunes.

- Become aware of the law of cause and effect, or karma. Every action has a reaction. If you're not happy with your life, make the changes you want to see, even during hard times such as job loss, bereavement, separation or illness.

- Let events come to you and stop provoking them. There is a time for everything. Observe yourself with clarity and detachment, and ask yourself if the effort is worthwhile.

- You are accountable. It is time to make peace with those you have hurt and ask for their forgiveness.

- Your errors in judgement lead to intolerance and harshness. Remember that others treat you as you treat yourself.

- Your life is filled with contradictions. It's time to clean up. You can then aspire to a much more harmonious life.

- You want to change the world and see justice done everywhere on the planet. Join an international movement or a humanitarian or social cause.

Keywords to Complete the Interpretation

- Honest and fair with integrity
- Fair and equitable

- Disciplined
- Methodical

- Wise and balanced
- Very organised and structured
- Great capacity for analysis and reflection
- Measures the scope of projects before taking action
- Tolerant
- Respects the rules
- Seeks balance and harmony
- Rigorous
- Meticulous
- Coherent
- Serious
- Impartial
- Obedient
- Sense of responsibility
- Logical mind

Reverse Card:

- Cold and austere
- Insensitive
- Inhibited personality
- Conservative
- Inflexible
- Strict
- Narrow-minded
- Unfair
- Picky
- Meticulous to the limit
- Critical
- Uncompromising
- Seeks quarrels
- Ill at ease
- Lack of enthusiasm
- Careful
- Easily unbalanced
- Confused
- Lack of ambition
- Likes to be on familiar ground, with no surprises or unforeseen events
- Need to follow a reassuring routine

- Straddling the rules
- Resentful
- Bureaucrat

- Fear of not succeeding, of making mistakes
- Protestant and rebellious

How to Integrate the Vibration of the Justice

To do so, one must learn to act with integrity in all areas of life. Life and its encounters will gradually shape you. It requires honesty, integrity and transparency to consciously choose what supports your evolution and reject what hinders it. Maintaining balance is important, though not always easy, as daily life constantly presents choices, temptations and challenges that test your judgement. Even with strong values, mistakes may still be made, and it is the individual's responsibility to acknowledge and learn from these mistakes.

Justice teaches us to take ownership of these outcomes and understand that our thoughts, intentions and actions determine the course of our lives. By consciously choosing how you respond, you can change your destiny. Misfortune does not come from heaven—your personal growth depends on embracing responsibility and becoming your most evolved self.

CHAPTER 9

THE HERMIT

The Hermit archetype calls for deep reflection and introspection. The answers lie within, but they can only be found by quieting the distractions that obscure the inner self. Once this is achieved, life begins to reveal its full meaning, offering guidance and showing the lessons and purpose that were previously hidden. This arcana emphasises two essential qualities needed to realise one's potential: disciplined action and selfless service to others. Both are needed to navigate the inner journey and develop the wisdom required for personal and spiritual growth.

However, the Hermit can also signify the avoidance of responsibility, withdrawal, or resignation from life. For some, it intensifies feelings of isolation, emptiness or low self-worth. In others, it manifests as constant busyness, overthinking or excessive rationalisation, leaving no room for emotion or genuine connection. This archetype challenges us to evaluate our priorities, confront the patterns that hold us back and extract the wisdom embedded in life's experiences. It encourages us to take a careful look inward in order to uncover the deeper truths about our path and purpose.

Characters

A teacher, a sage, a guide, an elderly person, a counsellor, a cautious or lonely person, a psychologist, a philosopher, a doctor, a pharmacist, a researcher, a scientist, a metaphysicist, a retiree, a bachelor, a monk, a mystic, a priest, a spiritual person, and a depressed, taciturn, or asocial person.

Personality

Qualities:

- Charitable
- Devoted
- Great humanist and sensitive to suffering
- Detached from the things of life
- Mature
- Wise
- Simple
- Humble
- Patient
- Discreet and not one to attract attention
- Introvert
- Difficult to grasp
- Tenacious
- Perfectionist
- Is interested in many things
- Thrifty and an outstanding financial planner
- Idealist who wants to save the world
- Dreamer
- Need for silence and order to flourish
- Need to be alone with oneself
- Need to express oneself
- Appreciates the little things in life
- Has a highly developed sixth sense
- Sensitive to the atmosphere around him
- Reserved and values his privacy
- Great intellectual skills

Faults:

- Miser
- Materialistic
- Thick-headed
- Mistrustful
- Sluggish
- Changing mood
- Secret, enigmatic and suspicious
- Doesn't admit contradictions
- Asocial
- Difficulty opening up to others
- Sensitive to rejection
- Folds in on itself
- Complex
- Chronic worry
- Excessively naive
- Strong propensity for self-analysis
- Greatly misunderstood
- Fallen idealist
- Confused and evasive
- Illogical lack of pragmatism
- Doesn't like to be rushed
- Difficulty adapting to change
- Lacks self-confidence and the ability to succeed
- Difficulty achieving aspirations
- Avoids problems and responsibilities
- Fear of facing life
- Vulnerable

Love Life:

- Loyal
- Patient
- Persevering
- Seeks peace and harmony
- Marriage is a serious commitment
- Must get to know each other before forming a couple

- Unconditional love
- Love is made up of many small gestures rather than great demonstrations of love
- Spiritual union
- Unites its destiny when trust is established
- Deep attachment based on inner qualities

Reverse Card in Relation to Love:

- Unfaithful
- Jealousy
- Wants to control their partner
- Uncompromising with regard to their partner
- Often changes partners
- Not very sentimental or romantic
- Egocentric
- Introverted and uncommunicative
- Not very demonstrative
- Constant need for reassurance
- Needs to feel loved
- Cerebral: love comes after everything else
- In a relationship for the sake of convenience, not love
- Lives a single life while having a life partner
- Often chooses to live alone as a result of disappointing relationships
- Dry heart

Professional Life:

- Discreet
- Reliable
- Persevering
- Needs to believe in what he does
- Prefers to work alone

- Disciplined
- Immersed in his work
- Perfectionist
- Spirit of synthesis and analysis
- Indispensable resource for colleagues
- Has a great understanding of the structure
- Attracted by humanitarian professions
- Strong interest in training abroad
- Planner and evaluator skills
- Logical
- Likes to expand his knowledge

Reverse Card in Relation to Career:

- Job loss, unemployment
- Victim of a budget cut
- Hurried retirement
- Stagnation
- Low remuneration
- Lack of motivation
- Asocial behaviour and difficulty communicating
- Overwhelming responsibilities
- Long-term projects that don't come to fruition
- Poor time management
- Dislikes having a stressful job with constantly changing demands
- Dry and thankless work that doesn't fulfil your aspirations
- Unrecognised skills
- Discouragement

Health:

- Long life
- Tames pain very early on
- Good resistance to disease
- Psychological weakness (depression, illness, nervous disorders, cyclothymia)

- The bone structure is his greatest weakness, causing rheumatism, joint pain associated with inflammatory phenomena, osteoarthritis, lumbago, and osteoporosis

- Aneurysm

- Stroke

- Insomnia

- Eating disorders (intoxication, anorexia, bulimia)

- Premature ageing (loss of teeth and skin elasticity, stiffness, and greying of the hair)

- Digestive disorders

The Hermit Applied to Your Daily Life

- You allow the demands of daily life to destabilise you. Now is the time to stop and take some time for yourself.

- Take a step back and reassess your priorities.

- You have always been at the service of others and forgotten yourself. Feed the desires that you had relegated to oblivion.

- Success and excessive materialism do not satisfy you. It's time to embark on an inner journey that will lead you to your destination.

- You are overwhelmed by the challenges you face. Take stock of your beliefs, values, morals, goals and ambitions.

- Stress and depression are waiting for you. Meditate on the reasons for these states of mind and how to lead a more fulfilling life.

- You wonder about life's great questions, and it is up to you to find the answers. Your time on Earth is limited.

- Chance encounters have changed your philosophy of life. Now is the time to pass on your valuable knowledge to those who are thirsty for it.

- Go on holiday alone and recharge your batteries in complete silence.

- You hear the call of the soul and nothing can stop you. Now is the time to give your life purpose.

- You fully enjoy your celibacy.

- Throughout your life, you have done your own thing and taken on many responsibilities alone. Today, accept the support and wise advice offered to you.

- Make the most of your retirement and stop blaming yourself. You have earned this money through hard work, so take ownership of it.

- Don't be like the grasshopper in La Fontaine's fable. Save money so you can enjoy your retirement.

- Slow down and take full advantage of what life has to offer. You no longer have to fight for what you want. You have been patient, and your efforts are now paying off.

- Your body is a temple. Take great care of it. Exercise and eat well to avoid illness. Also, respect your limits by getting at least seven hours' sleep per night.

Keywords to Complete the Interpretation

- Dedicated
- Discrete and reserved
- Clever
- Studious
- Scholar
- Reflexive
- Serious
- Sober and simple
- Careful
- Mature with great experience
- Patient
- Persistent
- Tenacious
- Economical
- Guide for others
- Need for solitude
- Inner work
- Meditative and mystical
- Deep and mysterious
- Humble

Reverse Card:

- Thick-headed
- Dogmatic
- Fearful
- Anxious
- Sad
- Austere
- Confused and illogical mind
- Miserable
- Mistrustful
- Asocial
- Passive; slow to react
- Tendency to self-analysis
- Doesn't like to be pushed around
- Difficulty adapting to change
- Rebel
- Unrealistic
- Hesitant and undecided
- Lack of boldness
- His fears prevent him from moving forward

- Misanthrope
- Timid
- Introvert, withdrawn
- Secret and enigmatic
- Impassive

- Feels misunderstood
- Fear of facing life
- Fear of loneliness
- Refuses to question himself

How to Integrate the Vibration of the Hermit

In order to do so, you must confront the reality of inner loneliness and accept it as part of the journey. Filling your life with distractions, activities or possessions cannot guarantee fulfilment or growth. This stage tests your willingness to release fears that limit your freedom, especially the fear of being alone, being judged, being rejected or being unloved.

By confronting these fears, you will be able to encounter your spiritual dimension and the questions that once troubled you will gradually give way to clarity and wisdom. You will realise that you do not need to conform to others' expectations to become the person you are meant to be. From this place of self-acceptance and insight, you can help others who may one day lose their way or struggle to find their path, just as you once did.

CHAPTER 10

THE WHEEL OF FORTUNE

The Wheel of Fortune archetype represents the primary cycles of life. It makes us aware of the choices and scenarios that shape our path. Like a wise teacher, it represents the lessons of transition, crisis, reward, and growth.

It also highlights the opportunities that life presents, which are not always seized. The most significant pitfalls are distraction, lack of direction, and repeating the same mistakes. However, if life is perpetual movement, it will eventually become necessary to raise one's consciousness and, as much as possible, stop exacerbating the pangs of fate!

Characters

An adventurer, a travel agent, someone with a malleable character, someone who takes charge of their life, an inventor, a speculator, a gypsy, a tramp, someone experiencing a great change in their destiny, an astrologer, someone involved in the divinatory arts, a stock exchange agent, a hypnotherapist, someone who suffers the vagaries of fate and an opportunist.

Personality

Qualities:

- Active
- Energetic
- Hates routine
- Always on the go
- Taste of adventure
- Looking for thrills
- Immediate satisfaction of the senses
- Savours the present moment
- Free and in control of his life
- Spontaneous
- Always in a good mood
- Eternal adolescent
- Carefree and bohemian
- Pleasure for life
- Instinctive behaviour
- Sense of initiative
- Charmer
- Good sense of humor
- Insightful
- Bold
- Versatile
- Resourceful
- Very clever
- Interested in everything
- Has many inner resources
- Great adaptability
- Takes a wholehearted approach to everything he undertakes
- Always has projects in mind
- Ready to fight for a cause close to their heart
- Deep anxiety about the future and the great metaphysical questions
- Knows how to surround himself well

Faults:

- Restless and unstable
- Nomadic and without ties
- Does not stay in one place
- Daredevil
- Careless
- Carefree and nonchalant
- Inconsistent, acts without thinking
- Dazed
- Goofy and tends to put their foot in their mouth without much thought
- Wants to go too fast
- Hates delays
- Influenceable
- Negligent
- Lack of motivation
- Proud
- Refuses any form of limitation or system that dictates his conduct
- Difficulty finding his place in society and discovering his true talents
- Has great insecurities
- Lives his life playing "double or nothing"; it's everything or nothing
- Undecided

Love Life:

- Very rich emotional life
- Likes being in love
- Joy for life
- Importance of renewal
- Doesn't complicate life
- Ability to be present
- Pays attention to the little things
- Likes to create surprises
- Lives day to day
- Willingness to do anything to make the relationship work
- Likes to travel as a couple
- Sentimental relationships are premeditated by karma

Reverse Card in Relation to Love:

- Superficial
- Opportunistic
- Frivolous
- Unstable
- One-day flings
- Ephemeral relationships
- Has a need for freedom and a fear of suffocation
- Independent
- Refuses to commit
- Sees his emotional life through rose-coloured glasses
- Difficulty managing emotions
- Will talk behind your back
- Must experience a constant rush of adrenaline; otherwise, the spark will dull

Professional Life:

- Versatile, a jack of all trades
- Creative
- Great know-how
- Ingenious
- Insightful
- Hates routine
- Likes travelling and commuting
- Good comprehension skills
- Aims for the top
- Great presence of mind
- Communication skills
- Excels in interviews
- Seizes opportunities as they arise
- Ability to stand out
- Rises through the ranks quickly
- Success in the professions of the future

Reverse Card in Relation to Career:

- Let's seize the opportunities that fate puts in our way

- Reversal of fortune

- Makes quick and poorly planned changes that can lead to loss, ruin, or bankruptcy

- Has difficulty obtaining job security and experiences professional instability

- Job loss

- Risk of tarnishing his reputation

- High staff turnover

- Ideas of grandeur and disproportion

- Stifling professional situation

- Accidents and dangers associated with road or rail travel

- Success is neither earned nor tainted by favouritism

Health:

- Very good health

- Needs to move

- Energetic

- Joint blockage (movements are difficult and painful)

- Poor blood circulation

- Stressed and restless

- Anguished and obsessed

- Stress-related insomnia

- Prone to fractures and bruises

The Wheel of Fortune Applied to Your Daily Life

- Everything around you is changing. You must decide whether to stay where you are or embrace change.

- You don't have to endure the pangs of fate. Achieve equanimity and serenity, especially when it comes to your emotional ups and downs.

- If you refuse to evolve and embrace your destiny and life project, your soul will regress in this life.

- Fate is knocking on your door and will not go away. Stop beating around the bush and make the right decisions.

- Respect the great cycles of life. There is no point trying to stop, speed up or push back time.

- Luck presents itself in many forms. Seize it!

- We are all connected. What you do to others, whether good or bad, you also do to yourself.

- No accident occurs unnecessarily. You have resisted change for too long. It's time to go in a different direction.

- A miracle is about to happen. Stay open to life's good graces.

- Make a commitment and do something useful with your life. Stop being passive and waiting in vain.

- If you are going through a very difficult situation and cannot see the light at the end of the tunnel, take a step back and you will find a solution. You are not your problem!

- Everything in life is cyclical. Choose when to be active and when to rest wisely.

- Open up to the unknown. Fate strikes where and when it wants, and being inflexible only makes things worse. Everything in this world is constantly changing, and you are no exception.

– Meditate on your karma and your place on Earth. Take stock of your strengths and weaknesses, and learn from all the significant events in your life.

Keywords to Complete the Interpretation

- Active
- Energetic and dynamic
- Taste for adventure
- Bold
- Combative
- Fortunate
- Curious and alert
- Creative
- Resourceful
- Versatile
- Great know-how
- Sense of initiative
- Clever
- Insightful
- Adaptable
- Good sense of humor
- Jovial and enthusiastic
- Spontaneous
- Lives day by day

Reverse Card:

- Careless; doesn't think about tomorrow
- Careless and carefree
- Inconsistent and irresponsible
- Wants to go too fast
- Runs badly calculated risks
- Negligent
- Opportunistic
- Playful
- Whimsical
- Marginal
- Influenceable
- Fearful

- Unstable, bohemian
- Daredevil
- Casino addictions
- Refuses limitations and refuses to conform to the norm
- Futile and superficial
- Tends to put their foot in their mouth
- Lacks motivation and is careless
- Faulty memory

How to Integrate the Vibration of the Wheel of Fortune

To do so, you must move in harmony with your personal evolution. Maintain balance in all areas of your life to avoid falling out of harmony. You are free to choose your path towards the destination set before birth. Depending on your choices, the law of cause and effect will either aid or hinder your progress. To evolve, you must embrace the unknown within you and embark on a journey of self-discovery.

Everyone must pass through cycles of transition, stagnation or crisis. The challenge lies in not getting lost in the cycle or fighting the current unnecessarily. Choices will present themselves, and wisdom lies in discerning the path offering the greatest learning opportunities. Everything evolves, and so must you. The greatest lesson is humility, because when we believe that we can control life entirely, fate swiftly adjusts the course regardless of our will.

Chapter 11

THE STRENGTH

The Strength archetype represents instinct, desire and the vital force that drives human existence. It symbolises the stage of self-mastery that distinguishes the ordinary from the evolved. This quiet force, present in everyone, is the seed of true victory and transformation. It is sustained by willpower, courage, perseverance and, above all, the power of love. Strength requires awareness and patience. It calls for the measured and conscious use of personal power, balancing passion with understanding, and instinct with reason.

However, when emotions are left uncontrolled, Strength can also reveal its shadow side. This can manifest as abuse, anger, violence or hatred, leading to a loss of direction and clarity. Such negativity fuels insecurities, creates unnecessary conflict and hinders growth. When we cling to attachments or resist change, our soul's evolution becomes compromised. Unchecked energy may turn inwards and become destructive, manifesting as aggression, impatience or hostility. This affects both personal well-being and relationships with others.

Characters

Leader, veterinarian, courageous person, social media influencer, artist, firefighter, sportsman or athlete, self-employed person, educator, lover, impulsive, passionate and independent person, ambassador and diplomat.

Personality

Qualities:

- Emotional
- Dedicated and caring
- Dynamic and energetic
- Not afraid to take on a challenge
- Great inner strength
- Total faith in his abilities
- Exceptional self-esteem
- Proud
- Valiant
- Courageous and determined
- Persevering
- Disciplined
- Great strength of character
- Ambitious
- Born leader who likes to dominate
- Lives intensely
- Reliable
- Spontaneous
- Curious
- Good sense of humor
- Joy for life
- Persuasive
- Idealistic
- Huge creative potential
- Fertile imagination
- Likes to be free and go on adventures
- Inspired, visionary and intuitive
- Constantly searching for the "Truth"
- Constantly in the heat of the moment

FAULTS:

- Angry and irritable
- Aggressive and violent
- Impatient
- Uncompromising
- Impulsive
- Hyperactive
- Resentful
- Proud
- Negative
- Eternally dissatisfied
- Unable to appreciate things and people for their true value
- Opportunistic
- Self-centered
- Paranoid
- Excessive taste for power, wants to own everything
- Poorly tolerates contradiction
- Needs to be admired and show off
- Sensitive to flattery
- Needs to justify oneself
- Refuses to question themselves
- Scattered
- Poor control of his emotions
- Tends to live in the future rather than the present
- Believes everything is due to his own efforts

Love Life:

- Passionate
- Romantic
- Dreamer
- Idealistic
- Exuberant
- Charismatic
- Seductive
- Sensual
- Diplomat
- Frank
- Only feels complete when he's in love or in a relationship
- Places great importance on love and friendship

Reverse Card in Relation to Love:

- Highly emotional

- Jealous

- Frivolous and libertine

- Domineering

- Manipulator

- Needs to please, to be loved and admired

- Seeks to satisfy his desires and impulses

- Confuses sexuality and deep feelings

- Conflicting relationships

- Tends to blame their partner for their own failures

- Passionate

Professional Life:

- Persevering

- Determined

- Ambitious and aims for a prestigious position

- Confident in their abilities

- Extensive know-how

- Self-taught

- Needs to surpass himself

- Passionate

- Needs to be recognised and appreciated for his skills

- Exercises authority with ease

- Knows success in all their endeavors

- Needs to be at the forefront of everything

- Professional life plays a leading role in their development

Reverse Card in Relation to Career:

- Blinded by disproportionate ambition

- Has difficulty making informed decisions due to impartiality

- Doesn't distinguish between personal challenges and competition

- Wishes to receive the honours immediately

- Complicates his life unnecessarily

- Invests his energy in lost causes

- Has difficulty taking orders

- Starts at the bottom of the ladder and moves up one rung at a time

- Likes to look good and be in the limelight

- Experiences imbalance due to overwork

- Will do anything to get a promotion

Health:

- Excellent health

- Great vitality

- Refuses to listen to his body

- Stress

- Exhaustion from overwork

- Heart failure

- Hypertension

- Nervous breakdown

The Strength Applied to Your Daily Life

– You have immense powers of persuasion. Use this gift to your advantage in any situation.

– Take the time to do things for yourself. Be creative and put your agenda aside for once!

– Let your heart do the talking and start a beautiful love story.

– We gain nothing by constantly competing with others. Recognise opportunities to learn from those around you and share your talents. Everyone will be a winner.

– Your life is lacking in tenderness. When it comes to seduction, let the other person take the first steps. Trust in life.

– Stop worrying about everything and nothing. Stay in the present moment. The answers will come to you intuitively.

– Find the child in you and see life as a game! You don't have to fight for anything.

– Your disproportionate ambitions hide a deep-seated lack of love. Be kind to others and to yourself.

– We gave you the gift of pedagogy. Pass on your joy for life, your passions and your knowledge to the next generation, who need it more than ever.

– Pride has no place in your daily life. You have nothing to defend or prove. May your life reflect the message you wish to convey.

– Learn to harness your potential and make it your own. Your greatest asset is your ability to generate creative ideas.

– The fear of displeasing others and of not being up to the task stifles your life. Dare to take risks and throw yourself into the adventure!

– Perfection is not of this world; otherwise, you would not be here. Give yourself permission to make mistakes, because that's how you learn and move forward.

– Play sports, move around, walk and breathe deeply. This is the most effective way to relieve stress!

Keywords to Complete the Interpretation

- Bold
- Powerful
- Determined
- Closed
- Imperturbable
- Knows how to overcome obstacles
- Doesn't fear hardships
- Great assurance
- Confident in their abilities
- Inner strength
- Strength of character
- Disciplined
- Persevering and determined to see things through to the end
- Power of persuasion
- Strong convictions
- Implied
- Courageous, brave, valiant
- Voluntary
- Cold-blooded
- Dynamic and energetic
- Great vitality
- Spirited
- Enthusiastic
- Radiant
- Magnetic and charismatic
- Captivating
- Original
- Proud
- Lives intensely
- Autonomous

Reverse Card:

- Aggressive
- Violent and brutal
- No self-control
- Hard and cruel
- Insensitive
- Irritable
- Authoritarian
- Uncompromising and inflexible
- Indomitable
- Abuses his power
- Invasive and suffocating

- Difficulty managing emotions
- Bubbly character
- Seeks out fights
- Snarling
- Resentful
- Vindictive
- Scattered
- Impatient
- Impulsive
- Arrogant
- Indifferent
- Proud
- Boastful

How to Integrate the Vibration of the Strength

To achieve this, you must first acknowledge your true self and recognise the ways in which anger and uncontrolled impulses influence or overtake you. Every day, you are faced with choices: peace or violence; compassion or envy; joy or grief; self-control or distraction. The events that unfold in your life reflect these decisions.

You are faced with these choices in your daily struggles, and the events that follow one another over the course of a day validate the merits of your decisions. For positive transformation to occur, you must put your ego aside, let go of yourself and embrace a much nobler cause. In doing so, you will be blessed with the power to become a better person every day of your life. At this stage of your evolution, pride makes way for an inner light — a consuming fire fuelled by love. Are you ready to take that evolutionary leap? If so, look within yourself to discover who you truly are. You will then intuitively know what you need to work on. Here, judgement has no place and only unconditional acceptance remains. Such is the power of strength within each of us!

Chapter 12

THE HANGED MAN

The Hanged Man archetype symbolises patience and surrender. There are times when neither moving forward nor retreating is possible, and waiting is the only option. During these times, it is important to allow events to unfold naturally. This stage requires faith, as patience is often overlooked in a society that values constant action. Although it may seem like a standstill or a trial, the Hanged Man indicates a need to pause, reflect, question and prepare for future challenges.

This arcana also speaks of trials, sacrifice and resignation. However, the danger lies in adopting the role of martyr and interpreting life as an endless struggle. The Hanged Man reveals the invisible prisons we create for ourselves, formed by limiting beliefs, rigid patterns and unhealthy attachments. His inverted position reminds us that he has chosen to be suspended, enduring the discomfort until realisation dawns. He teaches us that growth does not require suffering, and that liberation begins with a shift in perspective.

Characters

A servant, a slave, a depressed person, a drug addict, an alcoholic, an enlightened person or a mystic, a humanist, a yoga teacher, a healthcare worker, a victim, a seer, a disabled person, a volunteer, a dedicated person, and a disillusioned being.

Personality

Qualities:

- Friendly
- Fills others with little attention
- Deeply human
- Compassionate
- Great listening skills
- Soft
- Humble and freed from ego
- Helpful
- Generous
- Self-giving and altruistic
- Present in his community
- Possesses a spirit of sacrifice
- Very attached to those close to him
- Great safe, guide
- Simple
- Constantly seeks to surpass himself
- Visionary
- Intuitive
- Telepath
- Meditative
- Mystical
- High degree of spirituality
- Fascinated by the mystery of life

Faults:

- Egocentric
- Hypocritical
- Liar
- Manipulator
- Naive
- Devoid of critical thinking
- Dependent
- Suppresses his desires
- Sensitive in his skin
- Disillusioned and resigned
- Blinded by easy pleasures
- Refuses to grow up and learn from his mistakes
- Flees reality
- Blames others for his misfortunes
- Passive
- Powerless in the face of everyday challenges
- Low self-esteem
- Tendency to denigrate himself and devalue himself
- Afraid of disappointing others or not measuring up
- Eager to measure up in the eyes of others
- Feels like a victim
- Feelings of guilt

Love Life:

- Devoted
- Helpful
- Attentive
- Available
- Reserved and private in his relationships
- Radiant love
- Selfless, unconditional love
- Stands beside his partner and seeks their happiness
- Spiritual union with their loved one

Reverse Card in Relation to Love:

- A tumultuous, unfulfilling and sentimental life
- Searches in vain for their ideal partner
- Self-forgetfulness and sacrifice
- Lives through his partner
- Affective dependency
- Seeks to be indispensable
- Unable to say no
- Tends to idealise his partner
- Willing to do anything to keep their partner's love
- Wants to save his partner
- His small gestures often go unnoticed
- Lives in frustrating relationships that undermine his self-esteem

Professional Life:

- Inner growth and a job that nourishes the soul and the heart
- More motivated by happiness than remuneration
- Humanitarian professions
- Needs to be of service
- Needs to feel useful
- Doesn't like taking orders
- Hates routine chores
- Must take breaks during the day
- Knows the importance of a healthy atmosphere at work
- Hates competition and arguments

Reverse Card in Relation to Career:

- Lacks motivation and is stagnating
- Professional life is not a priority

- Works tirelessly for someone else's benefit
- Career that does not suit them
- Unhealthy atmosphere in the office, which undermines morale
- Everything is going too fast and he is finding it difficult to keep pace
- High level of absenteeism

- Working a 9-to-5 job, Monday to Friday, does not suit them
- Adheres to a non-traditional schedule
- High risk of depression
- Nebulous professional climate: he doesn't know what will happen to his position

Health:

- Must pay close attention to his health throughout his life
- Great sensitivity to everything around them
- Must avoid walkabouts
- Must learn to let go

- Difficulty coping with stress
- Fragile nervous system
- Prone to sickness and depression
- The importance of rest and calm

The Hanged Man Applied to Your Daily Life

- It's time to think about your own happiness, free from conflict. Whatever you do, you will be judged, but not by you.

- It is a delusion to believe that you have to suffer in order to progress in life. Change the way you think and your life will change too.

- Certainly, you are different from others, but that is no reason to feel excluded.

- Stop suppressing your desires and feelings. Express them freely.

- Know that there are times in life when you are not in control of your destiny. Accept your situation you are in and allow yourself to be guided by life's journey.

- Life is not a race against time. Take time to stop and clear your mind. This will prevent you from stressing yourself out and running around aimlessly.

- Wanting to control everything means missing all the little miracles in life. Embrace the unknown.

- Depression is the mismatch between dream and reality. Stop believing that you are subject to the vagaries of life. Be creative in the present moment and enjoy the results.

- Whether your trials are real or imagined, they will allow you to connect with your spiritual side.

- Even if it goes against popular belief, education or family values, free yourself from the chains holding you back so that you can be yourself. The freedom that follows is your greatest gift.

- Sometimes, to move forward, you have to turn around and try to understand the basis of your problems, because repeating the same mistakes without learning from them is the greatest danger.

- Self-giving is one of life's most beautiful gifts. Use it wisely. Indeed, it is in self-oblivion that the greatest moments of enlightenment occur — the pearls of our evolution.

- Pray, meditate and rest. This is the only way to recharge your batteries.

Keywords to Complete the Interpretation

- Selfless
- Helpful
- Generous
- Tolerant
- Dedicated
- Abandonment
- Let go
- Patient
- Docile
- Selflessness
- Self-forgetfulness
- Sacrifice
- Volunteering
- Charity
- Compassion
- Human
- Mission
- Idealistic
- Inspiration and creator of masterpieces
- Constructive and positive spirit
- Sensitive
- Gives little importance to material gratification
- Understands
- Ability to see the other side of the coin
- Transcendence
- Passions and socially high goals
- Very attached to his love
- Gives little attention to material gratification
- Must let go of the ego
- Clinical death
- Internal channel
- Sleep and premonitory dreams
- Astral travel
- Superior knowledge
- Intuitive, receptive and visionary
- Revelations and truths
- Strong karmic ties
- Telepathy
- Mystical

- Universal love
- Renounce earthly pleasure
- Very lofty, platonic ideals

- Prays
- Meditative silence
- Divine

Reverse Card:

- Egocentric
- Hypocritical
- Masochistic
- Sacrifice
- Humiliation and depreciation
- Exploitation and slavery
- Guilt and victimisation
- Emotional
- Dreamer
- Addiction (to games, drugs or alcohol)
- Affective dependency
- Lack of love
- Lack of critical thinking
- Lack of practicality

- Low self-esteem
- Difficulty loving oneself
- Disillusioned
- Fatalistic
- Discouraged
- Depressed
- Sickly
- Unstable
- Powerless
- Ineffective
- Inertia and resistance
- Bad will
- Unaware of the chains holding him down
- Difficulty saying no

How to Integrate the Vibration of the Hanged Man

In order to do so, you must learn to distinguish between dreams and reality. Life inevitably brings obstacles, tests and trials, but these experiences can act as catalysts for awakening. The Hanged Man directs your attention towards the hidden parts of yourself that have been rejected or denied. To evolve, you must confront these shadows, dispel illusions and accept that your challenges are integral to your personal growth. Although you may sometimes feel different from others, your greater purpose lies in breaking free from your inner constraints and discovering authentic freedom.

Like a Buddha in meditation, the Hanged Man invites you to suspend time, allowing realisations to arise from within. This requires identifying the inner voices that do not belong to you — those shaped by conditioning, fear or expectation. Once recognised, the long and patient work of deprogramming can begin. Though demanding, this process is essential for anyone seeking awakening and the path of self-discovery.

CHAPTER 13

THE DEATH

The Death archetype represents the end of a stage. To continue on their path and further their evolution, one must let go of everything that hinders progress and binds them to the past. The journey is marked by questioning, crises, mourning and unavoidable transitions, reminding us that nothing in this life is permanent and that everything is destined for transformation. As with the chrysalis that becomes a butterfly, the Death arcana urges us to avoid falling into routine and instead embrace the unknown. This surrender and letting go is essential in order to make room for something greater and entirely new.

However, the Dead also symbolise suffering of many kinds, as well as a refusal to grow, leading to a life filled with sorrow, regret and despair. When we believe ourselves to be victims of fate, our character hardens and resentment takes root until sadness becomes the norm. The danger lies in refusing to see yourself clearly as the author of your own suffering. Nevertheless, the law of life remains unchanging: we reap what we sow.

Characters

A victim, a person in mourning, a farmer, a geneticist, an archaeologist, an osteopath, a dying man, a forensic doctor, someone who wants to give up everything and start again, someone going through a period of great questioning.

Personality

Qualities:

- Serious and goes about his business
- Discreet, likes to go unnoticed
- Frank and direct
- Lucid
- Introverted
- Victim of social phobias
- Likes to argue and debate big questions
- Wholeheartedly defends his point of view
- Strong personality
- Upsets the established order
- Can be somewhat disturbing
- Thinks a lot before making a decision
- Awareness
- Hypersensitive
- Often feels lonely
- Nostalgic and melancholy
- Has a strong sense of belonging and is attached to the environment in which they were born
- Detached from material things
- Afraid of losing what he owns
- Fear of tomorrow and the unknown
- Love of life
- Intense life, little rest
- Overwhelmed by a permanent sense of urgency
- Always moving
- Wants to progress

- Doesn't look back, wants to get things done
- Questions the value of life and death and the cyclical nature of things

- Transformations and metamorphoses
- Courageous
- Takes responsibility for their choices

Faults:

- Rigid
- Cold
- Distant
- Indifferent
- Automaton, wanders aimlessly
- Skeptical and incredulous
- Mistrustful
- Bitter towards life
- Full of resentment
- Revolt and rebellious
- Rises against everything and nothing
- Feeling of persecution
- Paranoid
- Takes everything literally
- Blinded by fury
- Explosive temperament
- Angry

- Violent
- Frustrated
- Jealous
- Hateful
- Hostile
- Cynical
- Uncompromising
- Has difficulty keeping friendships
- Has difficulty opening up to others
- Uses depreciating words
- Negative
- Doesn't smile
- Represses his emotions
- Individualistic
- Anguish
- Misunderstood
- Fear of dying

Love Life:

- Has a lot to offer
- Gives all kinds of little attention to family and colleagues
- Has difficulty showing affection to a loved one
- Proximity is a source of shyness
- With time and patience, their heart will open up like a rose
- Trusting others and letting go can take several years

Reverse Card in Relation to Love:

- Cold and distant
- Solitary
- Individualistic
- Jealous
- Possessive
- Sarcastic and acerbic
- Condescending
- Uncompromising, critical of their partner
- Tyrannical
- Difficulty communicating
- Poor listening skills
- Satisfaction with immediate pleasures
- Must add a hint of whimsy to his love life
- Tries to guard against suffering by forming a shell

Professional Life:

- Meticulous
- Conscientious
- Leadership skills
- Passionate
- Intuitive
- Likes to think outside of the box

- Great analytical skills
- Good at carrying out investigations and asking questions

- Works in fields of interest (death, justice, ethical questions, the underground worlds, sexuality and the unconscious)
- Curious by nature

Reverse Card in Relation to Career:

- Radical changes at work
- Difficult times ahead and discouragement
- Negative attitude and disillusionment
- Chronic disease that undermines performance
- Anguish about the future
- Merciless, inhuman character
- Mortality in the workplace

- Distant relationships with colleagues
- Professional failure and stagnation
- Loss, ruin, bankruptcy, and the collapse of social status
- Victim of a negative entourage or corruption
- Payroll deduction and debts

Health:

- Health related to emotional well-being
- Skin diseases, such as shingles, psoriasis and eczema
- Stomach and intestinal disorders

- Bone disorders, such as osteoarthritis, arthritis and osteoporosis
- Joint pain and ligaments
- Herniated discs
- Chronic disease

The Death Arcana Applied to Your Daily Life

- A dark period is approaching. These events are intended to shake you up and encourage you to change your old ways and start afresh.

- Death or illness is creeping into your life and your daily routine will never be the same again. Your lifestyle will be completely transformed. However, you must resist the urge to block this new phase of development.

- Loneliness weighs heavily on you!

- Do not wait until you are bedridden or hospitalised before slowing down your hectic pace of life. You will soon be forced to rest.

- You can hardly let go of your past, which is preventing you from moving forward. It's time to live in the moment and let go of the ghosts that are keeping you from being happy.

- Many break-ups are to come, whether they are friendly, sentimental, professional or family-related. This is a sign that you are freeing yourself from the negative influence of certain people.

- Stop feeling sorry for yourself and overcome your lack of courage and willpower. Doing so will help you evolve much faster.

- You have no control over losses such as suicide, accidents, divorce or illness, which cause you pain. However, you can choose to either feel sorry for yourself or face life's big questions, thus initiating a genuine inner search that will shed more light on your place and purpose on Earth.

— It's time to let go of your materialistic life and turn to spirituality. This could involve volunteering or devoting yourself to a humanitarian cause close to your heart. Now is the time to focus on yourself.

— Your way of thinking prevents you from being happy. Get rid of destructive patterns and life scenarios that are no longer useful to you. Instead, dedicate your life to permanently cultivating happiness.

— Don't resist change. Remember that when one door closes, another opens to make room for something better!

— Stop complicating your life. Centre yourself in your heart, where you will find the answers to all your questions, and free yourself from your illusions. Life is prompting you to go back to basics and embrace the simplicity of things.

Keywords to Complete the Interpretation

- Active
- Structured
- Responsible
- Serious
- Direct, frank
- Effective
- Logic
- Lucid
- Sensible, perceptive

- Letting go
- Transformation, change
- Self-transformation
- Transition from youth to wisdom
- Radical transformation
- Strong will
- Doesn't look back, wants to progress
- Advances without fear or remorse

- Armored
- Persevering
- Decided
- Demanding of himself
- Strong personality
- Steadfast
- Power of decision
- Irrevocable decisions
- Great ability to detach
- Freed from the past

- Nostalgic
- Melancholy, sad
- Sense of belonging to their origins
- Feels alone and different from others
- Various interests
- Transitional life
- Realistic vision
- Losses
- Lives intensely, no time to waste

Reverse Card:

- Defeatist, fatalist
- Melancholic
- Fear of tomorrow and fear of the unknown
- Resigned
- Indifferent and detached
- Insensitive
- Represses their emotions and their feelings
- Hard on themselves and others
- Inflexible
- Uncompromising
- Incredulous and skeptical

- Hateful
- Resentful
- Violent
- Destructive nature
- Negative and demeaning words
- Enjoys ruining other people's dreams, portraying the negative side of things, and playing devil's advocate
- Lack of fantasy; too realistic
- Sadness
- Isolation

- Mistrustful
- Frustrated with life
- Stubborn
- Irrational
- Pretentious
- Individualistic
- Disturbing
- Cynical
- Fear of death

- Has difficulty opening up to others
- Easily discouraged
- Demoralised
- Pessimistic
- Prone to depression
- Paranoid
- Radical and hostile
- Breaks away from what is most important to him.

How to Integrate the Vibration of the Death

To integrate the vibration of death, you must first acknowledge and deeply explore your own suffering. It is time to release what no longer serves you, so you can set out in a new direction, standing on stronger ground. Even if you feel as though your world is falling apart or life is ending, it is not. This stage invites you to go beyond your own limits, whether real or self-imposed, and embrace deep, lasting transformation. The process will not be smooth, and you may get hurt along the way, but once the change is complete, you will be a different person. What feels like a nightmare today will, in fact, teach you profound lessons about life and yourself.

Whether you resist or try to escape this process, the truth will not change. It is a necessary part of life's great cycles. It gives you the chance to become a better person by inspiring you to confront your suffering and find the cause of the obstacles preventing you from moving forward and evolving in this life. However, to survive 'the grim reaper', it is best not to cling to the past, but to simply and humbly surrender to life and let time do its work.

THE TEMPERANCE

The Temperance archetype represents harmony within duality. She is the bridge between heaven and earth, reminding us that all human beings share the same origin and are interconnected. Temperance also symbolises the inner haven of peace that exists within each person, regardless of the surrounding storms. Gentle and protective, she acts as a guardian angel, watching over her followers and showing them the brightest path to follow — one that allows their souls to continue growing.

However, Temperance may also point to torpor, letting go or laziness. This reflects the tendency to wait in vain for life to resolve itself, as though decisions could be made on our behalf. However, failing to set a clear life goal can be dangerous. Temperance is not passive; it is an invitation to rebuild your strength and renew your confidence in yourself and in life. Avoiding responsibility does not aid personal growth. Instead, you must take stock of your life, assess your current situation, resist the urge for immediate gratification, and focus on achieving balance for peace, harmony, and joy.

Characters

A guardian angel, a friend, a mediator, a communication agent, a recreationist, an advertising agent, a therapist, an acupuncturist, a tourist or a vacationer, a massage therapist, an electrician, a human relations counsellor, and a healer.

Personality

Qualities:

- Generous
- Available
- Benevolent
- Compassionate
- Helpful
- Soft
- Doesn't try to attract attention
- Distant (especially in childhood)
- Extremely sensitive
- Patient
- Accommodating
- Good adaptation capacity
- Diplomat
- Communication skills
- Natural motivator
- Magnetic
- Has an easy time forming friendships
- Defends humanitarian or ecological causes
- Sensitive to pollution and all forms of aggression
- Peacemaker
- Seeks calm and harmony
- Need for silence
- Avoids problems and conflicts
- Importance of art (song, dance and music)
- Lives one day at a time
- Serenity of the moment
- In harmony with the cycles of nature
- Glowing aura

- Angelic
- Pleasant
- Refined
- Gift of healing the sick
- Ability to perform miracles
- Likes outings and activities
- Sensitivity to the high vibrations of the soul
- Ability to communicate with guides
- Likes to have fun

Faults:

- Idle
- Lazy
- Indifferent
- Influenceable
- Messy
- Careless
- Disoriented
- Unstable employment and frequent moving
- Hyperactive
- Fashion victim
- Spender
- Lack of personality
- Unable to take a stand
- Keeps changing their mind
- Plagued by many insecurities
- Unable to sit still
- Difficulty taming solitude and silence
- Too sociable
- Fear of displeasing others
- Spends her life making others happy and forgets her real priorities
- Unable to say no
- Without specific goals in life
- Shuns responsibilities
- Delays everything until the last minute
- Waits for things to work out on their own
- Reflects on her misfortune

Love Life:

- Very favored sentimental life
- Has a lot to give
- Sincere
- Tender
- Generous
- Soft
- Takes an interest in her partner's life
- Communication is important to her
- Affectionate
- Opening of the heart
- Sincere and lasting love
- Knows how to keep the flame alive
- Seeks harmony in love and friendship
- Believes that sexuality is a sweet sharing experience
- Avoids arguments

Reverse Card in Relation to Love:

- Indifferent
- Cold
- Difficulty separating love and friendship
- Lack of communication
- Refuses to open up to love
- Hurt by heartache
- To love means to suffer
- Represses some form of bisexuality

Professional Life:

- Eager to learn
- Needs to be stimulated
- Likes to pass on knowledge
- Ease of speaking in public
- Adaptability
- Phenomenal intuition

- Very sociable
- Likes to exchange, share, and discuss

- Field of spirituality
- Alternative medicine
- Outstanding communicator

Reverse Card in Relation to Career:

- Jealous of the talent of others
- Indifferent, does nothing interesting
- The end justifies the means, ready to pay the price
- Intolerant of the ideas of others
- Routine and frustrating work, monotonous tasks
- Dishonest partner

- Inability to concentrate; scattered
- Communication with colleagues does not go well
- Agitation, stress, and unnecessary anxieties
- Results are not as high-quality as desired
- Incompetent and opportunistic

Health:

- Health and outlook on life are closely linked
- Very energetic
- Ability to heal themselves and heal others
- Hypersensitive

- Stress
- Anxiety
- Nervousness
- Subject to depression and overwork

- Captures the synergies that surround it

- Fragile nervous system

- Age-related weaknesses (circulatory system, arteries, bladder, kidneys)

- Chronic fatigue

The Temperance Applied to Your Daily Life

- Calm returns after the storm. Take this opportunity to rest and rebuild your strength.

- A miracle has just happened in your life, but you haven't noticed it yet. We are watching over you.

- You can't always be right. Be flexible and find a possible compromise. Remember, there are always two sides to every story.

- Calling in a mediator is probably the best solution, as you and your opponent are stuck in your positions and unable to communicate.

- Treat yourself to a health retreat to rebalance all aspects of your being.

- Stress undermines your life. This is why you cannot concentrate and make careless mistakes. Sign up for yoga or meditation classes to find peace of mind and 'get out of your head'.

- It's time to start questioning the meaning of your life. To do so, you must strike a balance between the material and the spiritual. This will be your real challenge!

- Stop trying to please everyone and be yourself. Find your true nature and stay true to your core values.

- Take your rightful place. You will not evolve by erasing yourself or buying peace.

- Certainly, you have great intellectual aptitude, but you would benefit from using your remarkable intuition more. Trust yourself!

- Your guardian angel is watching over you. Feel his presence and energy. He is protecting and guiding you right now. Silence yourself internally and you will be able to hear his message. Watch out for any signs he might send you.

- Those around you seek your company because you are so sensitive to the suffering and problems of others. You have a healing gift.

- You are a natural communicator. Your calm nature, wisdom and great learning inspire and motivate others.

Keywords to Complete the Interpretation

- Calm
- Soft
- Kind
- Adaptability
- Accommodating and flexible
- Conciliatory
- Balance
- Easy to live with
- Ability to motivate others
- Wishes to pass on their knowledge
- Technologies and communications
- Ecologist
- Environmentalist
- Pacifist and non-violent

- Patient
- Diplomat
- Altruistic
- Benevolent
- Compassionate
- Indulgent
- Loyal
- Magnetic
- Playful
- Good communicator
- Follows the rhythm of the sun

- Serenity
- Harmony
- Avoid problems and conflicts
- Life of the party
- Likes to be entertained
- Arts (dance, music, singing)
- Lives one day at a time
- Sabbatical leave
- Vacation
- Vegetarianism
- Miracles

Reverse Card:

- Cold
- Indifferent
- Let it go
- Idle, passive
- Lazy
- Unbalanced
- Unsuitable
- Impressionable
- Influenced, malleable
- Fashion victim

- Negligent
- Carefree
- Restless
- Unstable
- Changing as the weather
- Thoughtless
- Devoid of personality
- Maintains prejudice
- Forgets about worries while having fun

- Superficial
- Careless
- Spender
- Lives in the past

- Minimising problems and their importance
- Delays everything overnight

HOW TO INTEGRATE THE VIBRATION OF THE TEMPERANCE

To do so, you must first pause and take a break from constant physical and mental activity. Only then will you realise how much of yourself you have neglected. Consider how your inability to say no, your aversion to solitude, your tendency to prioritise others and your readiness to change yourself for the sake of others' approval have shaped your path. Open your eyes to this truth.

This moment of rest is a blessing, providing an opportunity to reflect on the journey ahead and, more importantly, the changes you must embrace to grow as an individual. Do not be afraid, for this oasis of calm after the storm is often accompanied by unexpected miracles. More than at any other stage of life, it is during times of restraint that your guardian angel can quietly reveal their presence quietly, offering you guidance and protection without you realising. This pause comes after your soul has faced great trials, and it is precisely this state of fragility that brings angelic help closer. Once optimism, confidence and serenity return, you will be far better equipped to face the challenges ahead and respond to life with wisdom. The past, then, serves only one true purpose: to stop you from making the same mistakes again. By this stage, you will have learned important lessons — at least until the next challenge inevitably appears on the horizon.

CHAPTER 15

THE DEVIL

The Devil archetype represents the darker aspects of human nature, such as impulses and temptations, that we often try to conceal. The Devil feeds on fears, vices, wounds, and weaknesses, and through the desire for power and money, keeps beings in a state of slavery.

This arcana forces people to confront their shadow side, along with the prejudices and perceptions they project onto others. Driven by obsession, passion, and unbridled energy, the Devil seeks only to satisfy his desires, whether through the body, sexuality, power, or material pleasures. Taking responsibility for his actions is not one of his strengths. Here, pride reigns supreme.

Characters

A hypnotist, a warlord, a surgeon, a thief, a banker, an athlete, a charismatic person, an occultist, an ambitious and passionate person, a chef or restaurateur, a manipulative person, someone with power, a sexual pervert, and a wealthy person.

Personality

Qualities:

- Very energetic
- Passionate
- Fiery
- Creative
- Complex
- Emotional
- Whole
- Charmer
- Magnetic
- Likes to be the center of attention
- Never goes unnoticed
- Likes to be admired
- Guided by instincts and impulses
- Carnal and sensual
- Knows how to achieve their goals
- Likes to taste and touch everything
- Nice company
- Unparalleled host
- Joy for life
- Epicurean and fun-loving
- Knows how to make the most of life
- Likes to laugh, have fun and party
- Benefitted by capitalism
- Knows how to grow their assets
- Importance of material goods and luxury items
- Success requires the possession of many goods
- Never goes unnoticed

Faults:

- Self-centered
- Egocentric
- Manipulator
- Liar
- Profiteer
- Possessive
- Jealous
- Envious
- Has trouble enjoying the happiness of others
- Destroys others physically, psychologically, emotionally and financially
- Megalomaniac
- Aggressive (gestures and words)
- Always on the defensive
- Obsessed with money, power and sexuality
- Perversion, deviation and lust
- Corruption
- Sensitive to flattery
- Disturbing
- Seeks to be the center of attention
- Inner duality
- Unstable, goes from one extreme to the other
- Refuses to see themselves as they are
- Money is a symbol of power and a way of measuring yourself against others
- Defends their possessions and assets
- Guided by greed
- Avoids problems by going overboard
- Ignores their limits
- Dependence (on drugs, tobacco, alcohol, sex, money, compulsive gambling, gluttony and emotional dependence)
- Subject to split personality, schizophrenia, neurosis and psychosis
- Attracted to witchcraft, Satanism, black magic and mediumship
- Paranoid

Love Life:

- Passionate
- Sensual
- Seducer
- Likes to capture the attention of loved ones
- Needs to be loved in return
- Seeks to maintain or rekindle the flame
- Love unites his inner duality
- Gives a lot of importance to the physical appearance of his partner
- Sexual

Reverse Card in Relation to Love:

- Jealous
- Frivolous and libertine
- Unfaithful
- Difficulty having a stable relationship
- Refusal to commit
- Difficulty opening the heart
- Conflictual relationship
- Codependency
- Animal instinct
- Difficulty distinguishing between physical needs and love
- To love is to possess the other
- Abuse and physical and psychological violence (perpetrator or victim)
- Unbridled sexuality

Professional Life:

- Clever
- Competent
- Passionate
- Motivated

- Initiative
- Meticulous
- Devoted
- Bold
- Determined

- Born organiser
- Sense of command (management positions)
- Seeks to reach the top

Reverse Card in Relation to Career:

- With an explosive character
- Energy focused solely on professional activity
- Attracted by gain
- Self-centered
- A manipulator, ready to do anything to achieve their goals
- Heightened emotions
- Physical and psychological abuse and blackmail

- Covets prestigious positions
- Bad influence from colleagues
- Workaholic and careerist
- Corruption and deception
- Infidelity (sexual relations with a co-worker)
- Closed to any dialogue
- Seduced by the hierarchy and abusing power

Health:

- Excellent health
- High resistance to disease
- Weak points in sexual health (e.g. frigidity, erectile dysfunction, infertility)

- Tendency to gain weight with age
- Hypertension
- Cardiovascular problems

- Psychic disorders (neurosis, psychosis, schizophrenia, megalomania, madness, obsession, nervous imbalance and repression of homosexuality)

- Fragility of the reproductive system

- Cancer

- Diseases of the digestive system (stomach, ulcers, constipation, intestinal calculus, ulcerative colitis and Crohn's disease)

- Sexually transmitted and blood-borne infections (STBBIs)

The Devil Applied to Your Daily Life

– Stop trying to control the people around you. This suggests that you have low self-esteem and little respect for yourself.

– You are the victim of someone's bad intentions around you who seems to take pleasure in manipulating and making you suffer. Wake up and take back control of your life!

– Your partner is unfaithful to you.

– Ambition destroys its master. See how much you have become his slave.

– You suffer from chronic dissatisfaction. Try to understand why you can no longer enjoy life's little pleasures.

– Passions and desires of all kinds dominate your life. However, they will never be fully satisfied. It is up to you to rebalance your inner self and find lasting happiness.

– The occult, magic and mediumship fascinate you. Remember that these methods do not guarantee a better life as they are not accompanied by a high vibration. There is no magic bullet. Sooner or later, you will have to face your problems.

— You pay inordinate attention to your physical appearance, such as fashion, bodybuilding, hairstyles and cosmetic surgery. These obsessions can reinforce your illusions and lead to profound self-doubt and shame. Love yourself for who you are!

— It's time to think about the consequences of your actions. Lust, money, parties and unbridled sexuality will lead to soul regression sooner or later.

— It is up to you to choose between good and evil. One will lead you to a life filled with crises, struggles and trials. The other will help you to surpass yourself.

— Selfishness and pride are two flaws you must overcome in this life. There is no miracle solution. You must cultivate selflessness and open your heart to others.

— Stop seeing everything in black and white and imagining the worst possible scenarios. Your negative thoughts create your reality. Change your attitude and watch the miracle unfold before your eyes.

Keywords to Complete the Interpretation

- Charismatic and bewitching
- Never goes unnoticed
- Hypnotic
- Eloquent
- Unifying, meditating and creative will
- Self-centered
- Proud

- Whole
- Coherent
- Active
- Impulsive
- Ardent and fiery
- Intense
- Passionate
- Joy for life
- Desire
- Eroticism and sexuality
- Pleasure of the senses
- Emotional
- Complex
- Universal and non-judgemental, understanding

- Power
- Manipulator
- Corruption
- Destruction
- Angry and aggressive
- Poor self-control
- Jealous
- On the defensive
- Money
- Materialistic
- Obsessed with food or alcohol
- Sexual drives and instincts
- Panic
- Black magic

Reverse Card:

- Authoritarian and domineering
- Tyrannical
- Angry
- Abusive
- Bad

- Lust
- Carnal
- Perverse
- Pleasures and thrills
- Slave to their senses

- Aggressive, violent and brutal in gestures and words
- Boiling character
- Spirit of vengeance
- Spirited
- Unstable
- Overexcited
- Hysterical
- Greedy
- Wants to do everything at once
- Animality
- Impulsiveness
- Lack of restraint
- Doesn't know their limits
- Epicurean
- Flattery, likes to be admired
- Irresistible charm
- Love games
- Sect guru
- Dependence (sex, alcohol, tobacco, drugs, money, compulsive gambling, food, emotional dependence)
- Self-centered
- Narcissistic
- Calculator
- Manipulator
- Power freak
- Pretentious
- Lure of profits
- Possessive
- Takes and receives, rarely gives
- Attracted by what shines
- Creates false needs
- False spirituality
- Desecration of the sacred
- Satanism
- Black witchcraft

How to Integrate the Vibration of the Devil

To truly embrace this vibration, you must dare to look within and confront your darkest self. This is the stage of temptation, where desires of every kind call out to you. The fear of suffering can make it easy to surrender completely to immediate pleasures, whether through sexuality, materialism, power, food or the way we see and present our bodies. In such moments, instinct takes precedence over reason and the ego reigns supreme. However, anyone who believes they are in control will soon find themselves enslaved instead. The Devil is not just a personal struggle; it is deeply woven into our civilisation today. We see it in newspapers, on television, in films, in politics, in education, and even in the games and hobbies that are supposed to entertain us. We kill in the name of God while entire nations go hungry so that profit can be preserved.

Whether you realise it or not, the Devil confronts you with your own duality. When the time comes to choose, which will you embrace: shadow or light? This archetype calls on you to rise above unchecked passion, desire and obsession. It asks you to recognise the illusions that bind you and make you believe that they sustain you. The way forward is to overcome division, addiction, anger and frustration by opening your heart. By choosing this path, you will overcome the challenges you face and release the heavy karmic burden you came into this life to clear. Remember this always: only love has the power to heal.

CHAPTER 16

THE TOWER

The Tower archetype represents crisis, upheaval and the sudden changes that are an inevitable part of life. It is a time of profound reflection, when the pillars of our existence are shaken. Loss of status, reversal of fortune and painful shocks occur, but they serve a hidden purpose. These disturbances break down rigid patterns and force us to abandon old habits that hinder our growth. Once the storm has passed, a new awareness emerges, bringing liberation and relief.

The Tower also reflects our refusal to see ourselves truthfully. When we are blinded by vanity, pride and excess, we make mistakes and face consequences that feel like 'divine wrath'. The lesson is clear: we must embrace change and renewal instead of clinging to harmful cycles that repeat endlessly. If we resist, life itself will intervene to awaken us.

Characters

An entrepreneur, an immovable agent, a meteorologist, an airplane pilot, a genius, a construction worker, an inventor, an architect, a marginal person, a seismologist, a mason, a minister, a leader of a multinational company, a trade unionist, a revolutionary, a programmer, and an analyst.

Personality

Qualities:

- Tolerant
- Empathetic
- Frank
- Proud
- Confident
- Healthy self-perception
- Awakened mind
- Great intellectual qualities
- Inspiring
- Ambitious: aim high and reach for the stars
- Bold and fearless
- Conqueror
- Great builder
- Persevering
- Courageous
- Whole character
- Defends their point of view
- Transmits their knowledge
- Endowed with multiple talents
- Unpredictable
- Instinctive
- Wants to be appreciated
- Sensitive to the opinions of others
- Likes taking on challenges
- Wants to be at the heart of the action
- Experiences many upheavals
- Thirst for freedom
- In love with the absolute
- Defends great causes
- Wants to change beliefs and the established order
- Wants to change collective consciousness
- Affirms differences
- Creator of their own happiness
- Creative

Faults:

- Self-centered
- Proud
- Sufficient
- Domineering
- Contemptuous
- Condescending
- Impatient
- Susceptible
- Stubborn
- Categorical
- Makes no compromises
- Thinks they have the truth
- Disconnected from reality
- Runs away from everyday life
- Obsessive delusions
- Lazy
- Exploiter
- Abuses good things
- Doesn't question himself
- Megalomania, grandeur and madness
- Difficulty collaborating and communicating with others
- Attempts to undermine the happiness of others
- Distrustful and unable to trust anyone
- Skeptical
- Impulsive
- Imprudent
- Reckless
- Explosive character
- Revolt
- Stands up against authority figures
- Narrow-minded
- Sensitive to flattery
- Importance of hierarchical status
- Reversal of fortune

Love Life:

- Passionate
- Likes to take the first steps
- Great moments of happiness
- Assertive and self-confident
- Union where individual freedom takes precedence
- Wishes to have children at the start of their union
- Wishes to get married quickly
- Sudden transformations and changes in the couple's lives
- Love at first sight

Reverse Card in Relation to Love:

- Pitfalls and trials
- Twists and turns (misfortunes, failures, ruptures and questioning)
- Unhealthy balance of power
- Relationship dominated by money and power
- Manipulator
- Egocentric
- Jealousy
- Angry
- Quarrelsome
- Aggressive
- Physical or psychological violence
- Disrespectful

Professional Life:

- Ambitious
- Focused on specific objectives
- Keen intelligence
- Business expansion
- Sees far and wide
- Frequent job changes
- New departures
- Career reorientation
- Awakening of consciousness
- Avant-garde

- Has brilliant ideas
- Modernity, uses cutting-edge technology

Reverse Card in Relation to Career:

- Rushing, impulses
- Impulsive and reckless
- Obstinate
- Unstable moods
- Dissatisfied and very critical
- Dislikes taking orders
- Many pitfalls that prevent progress
- Self-pity and feeling that circumstances are unfair
- Ideas of grandeur
- Attracted by material goods
- Seeks to climb the ladder quickly
- Professional failure
- Is refused a promotion
- Declines a social position
- Unexpected changes and a need for freedom

Health:

- Minor health problems
- Longevity
- Unpredictable health
- Subject to accidents of all kinds
- Spasms and tics
- Burns, bruises and fractures
- Stroke
- Rash symptoms
- Nervous and emotional shocks

The Tower Applied to Your Daily Life

- You have reached a point of no return. The major changes happening in your life right now will benefit you in the long term. They will enable you to rebuild your future on much more solid foundations.

- Do not let hardship overwhelm you, even if the circumstances seem unfair. Lasting happiness awaits you at the end of the road.

- You caused the failures you face today yourself. Above all, don't try to recreate what has been destroyed. Instead, cultivate humility and let go. You are in a period of transition.

- It's time to change the way you think. Stop burying your head in the sand and recognise your flaws and weaknesses.

- Go towards novelty and change. To evolve, you have to take risks! Embrace your freedom and the myriad new adventures that await you.

- The deep crisis you are currently experiencing (illness, job loss, bankruptcy, open conflict, etc.) will expose your vulnerability. It shows you that you are not the person you thought you were. Embrace this change in your destiny and don't resist it.

- You experience nervousness and anxiety because you are afraid of losing control of your life. Let time do its work. Remember that you have the power to give direction to your life. Allow yourself to be guided through these unstable times.

- Everything is crumbling around you, and you feel misunderstood. The problem is that you have created an illusory sense of security for yourself. The crisis you are experiencing tells you what you need to do to change, even if it feels like you are leaping into the void.

— You are experiencing a second adolescence, a period of rebellion, which will lead you towards happiness and spiritual growth. Ambition and money are no longer sufficient sources of motivation. This is where real personal growth begins.

— You stubbornly cling to your certainties, opinions and beliefs. This approach is not scalable to the soul. Set yourself goals and plans that you have never dreamed of before and get started!

— Meditate on your inner prisons and consider how power, ego, money and success have made you believe that you are free.

Keywords to Complete the Interpretation

- Ambitious
- Bold
- Determined
- Great willpower
- Effective
- Builder
- Conqueror
- Intrepid and brave
- Aim for the top
- Likes taking on challenges
- Wants to succeed
- Proud
- Reserved
- Thirst for the absolute
- Powerful
- Thinks big
- Creator of their own happiness
- Ascent and fall
- Upheavals
- Fast transformations
- Unexpected success (social, financial, etc.)

- Not easily discouraged by failure
- Frank
- Defends their identity
- Philosopher and intellectual
- Great mental qualities
- Enlightened awareness
- Open-mindedness
- Self-love
- Healthy self-perception

- Great survival instinct
- Close to nature
- Coronation
- Titles, degrees and diplomas
- Interior elevation
- Gives a spiritual twist to their life
- Released from the material world
- Worthy

Reverse Card:

- Selfish
- Pretentious and conceited
- Proud
- Inordinate ego
- Envious
- Authoritarian
- Categorical
- Dogmatic
- Distrustful, skeptical and suspicious
- Contemptuous
- Narrow-minded
- On your mind

- Impulsive
- Impatient
- Reckless
- Inordinate ambition
- Hierarchical status
- Delirium
- Megalomaniac and madness of grandeur
- Craftsman of his own misfortune
- Feelings of guilt
- Locked up, needs air and light

- Domineering
- Aggressive
- Angry and violent
- Revolt
- Rise against all authority
- All-powerful
- Persecution
- Frustrations
- Loss and destruction

- Takes refuge in a wave parallel (abuse)
- Self-destructive tendencies
- Dispossessed of personal power; wants to be considered
- Exploitative and abusive profit
- Possession
- Material wealth
- "Lightning" from the sky
- Susceptible

How to Integrate the Vibration of the Tower

To integrate the vibration of the Maison Dieu, you must place less importance on appearance. Most importantly, you must let go of your sense of achievement and security. In life, everything can fall apart without warning. It is an illusion to believe that you are in full control of your life and immune to tragedy. Indeed, nobody knows if they will lose their job, fall seriously ill, be abandoned by their spouse or have their house washed away in a flood or burned down tomorrow.

As long as you insist on controlling everything, you will face repeated trials. Mistakes will be repeated and growth will stall. Instead, learn to take risks with clarity and foresight, as this is the foundation of true success. Accept the need to change before circumstances force you to. Life is movement; life is transition. Embrace the wind of change and remember that the only constant is change. As Socrates reminds us, falling down is not the same as failing. Failure is refusing to get back up again.

Chapter 17

THE STAR

The Star archetype emphasises the importance of self-love and self-care. It teaches that true happiness comes from within, rather than from material possessions or other people. To be happy, it is not necessary to escape or be distracted; life simply needs to be less complicated. This card calls for complete openness of consciousness, bringing the soul's most luminous qualities to the fore. It is a guiding light that illuminates the path ahead. Like a pure and innocent child, the Star holds nothing back — there is no need to hide, fear or repress anything.

However, the Star can also highlight inner disharmony. When you feel disoriented, misguided or embittered by the world's wickedness, the greatest challenge is to silence your inner critic and avoid letting negativity dominate your perspective. Without courage and willpower, you can quickly become disillusioned and torn by internal conflict. To regain your self-esteem, you must set yourself goals and achieve your dreams. Then, you can believe in a bright future.

Characters

A model, a person of good appearance, a musician, a person who meditates, a hairdresser, an herbalist or phytotherapist, a craftsman, an antique dealer, a landscaper, a gardener, a poet or a writer, a massage therapist, an interior designer, a minimalist, and a beautician.

Personality

Qualities:

- Endearing
- Imbued with softness and delicacy
- In harmony with oneself
- Sensitive
- Not pretentious
- Endowed with natural goodness
- Generous
- Attentive
- Empathetic
- Dedicated
- Great listening skills
- Available
- Friendly
- Integrated
- Frank and sincere
- Modest
- Dreamer
- Idealistic
- Thirst for fairness
- Not inclined to compete with others
- Friend of nature
- Quality of life
- Live in the present moment
- Purity of soul
- Illuminated from the inside
- Confident in his destiny
- Protected by his lucky star
- Spiritual and attached to inner life
- Attracted by the universal language and its symbols
- Gift of clairvoyance

- Pacifist
- Filled with hope
- Endowed with a vivid imagination
- Optimistic

- Intuitive and visionary
- Interested in the great mysteries of life
- In search of truth

Faults:

- Destabilised
- Melancholic
- Disillusioned with life
- Resigned
- Passive
- Disoriented
- Prone to depressive episodes
- Wants to please everyone
- Unable to say no
- Self-forgetfulness
- Inner fragility
- Lack of perseverance and determination
- Lack of courage
- Prisoner of their ivory tower
- Asocial
- Looks inward
- Lack of spontaneity

- Unrealistic
- Prisoner of his chimeras and illusions
- Unable to distinguish the useful from the futile
- Lies to avoid hurting loved ones
- Sensitive to rejection, criticism
- Naïve and gullible
- Has difficulty detecting questionable situations and shady characters
- Victim of profiteering and malicious individuals
- Puts his foot in his mouth
- Let the opportunities slip by
- Unreasonable fears

- Embittered by human wickedness
- Difficulty living in the present moment

Love Life:

- Predestined love
- Family-oriented
- Sincere relationships
- Stable and lasting love
- Romantic
- Affectionate
- Present
- Attentive
- Loyal
- Generous
- Beautiful inside and out
- Blossoming
- Sweet
- Compassion
- Happiness
- Harmony
- Availability
- Listening ear
- Knows how to reassure and advise loved ones
- Wonderful friend
- Unparalleled host

Reverse Card in Relation to Love:

- Repetitive failures
- Permanent depressive state
- Possessive
- Cold
- Distant
- Insincere feelings
- Sentimental disillusionment
- Naive
- Refuses to be loved
- Rejection of femininity and motherhood
- Male homosexuality
- Unavailable and indifferent

Professional Life:

- Humanitarian profession
- Must feel useful
- Good listening skills
- Ease of working in a team
- Seeks harmony
- Sensitive to arguments
- Inventive spirit
- Does not seek fame or competition

- Little focus on performance results
- Work-life balance
- Needs a job that nourishes their soul
- Needs a peaceful place to rebuild their strength
- Visionary and intuitive
- Creative

Reverse Card in Relation to Career:

- Fear of displeasing and of not being up to the task
- Tendency to underestimate oneself
- Does not seek to develop professionally
- Lack of will and ambition
- Is exploited and their naivety is taken advantage of
- Melancholy mood that attracts little sympathy
- Can't say no

- Holds a job that is not a sufficient source of income
- Holds a position whose future is uncertain
- Lack of autonomy and initiative
- Job is not fulfilling
- Desperate and shuns responsibilities
- Their dreams and hopes fall apart

Health:

- Good health in general

- Biological clock adjusted to the quarter turn

- Emotional health problems

- Must avoid toxic situations (gossip, slander, arguments, unhealthy places and overcrowded cities)

- Sensitive to pollution and chemicals

- Special attention to the reproductive system (uterus, menstrual cycle, hormones)

- The body goes into automatic shutdown mode at the slightest virus

- Water therapy and thermal cures

- Give yourself time to recover

The Star Applied to Your Daily Life

- Don't let the critics get you down. Focus on your positive attributes because you only have one life to live!

- You have many talents waiting to be discovered. Why not sign up for music or art lessons?

- Rent a cottage by the water and take a few days to relax. It's time to get closer to nature.

- Your nervous system is fragile, so take care of it. Meditate or listen to the silence within to free yourself from daily stress. It will re-energise you.

- Does your life reflect what you imagined, or has it become an intolerable race against time? Get back to basics by adhering to the principles of voluntary simplicity.

- By always trying to please others, you have ended up forgetting yourself and putting your dearest dreams aside. Create a list of your short-, medium- and long-term goals, and achieve one of them before the end of the month!

- You have sensitive skin. Why not listen to your heart and stand up for abused animals, children or the frail elderly, or support another cause close to your heart?

- Life has endowed you with many talents. Put them to good use! Pass on your knowledge and skills to as many people as possible by developing your skills as a teacher, writer, coach or public speaker. You will seduce the crowds.

- Find your feminine side and welcome the love growing inside you. If appropriate, consider having children. Parenting is certainly part of your life plan.

- You tend to let yourself be overwhelmed by the obstacles in front of you. Roll up your sleeves and face these trials with courage and determination. This will be your biggest challenge.

- You are very sensitive to the omnipresent violence around you. Do your best to restore peace without playing the victim.

- Spirituality is part of your daily life. It is your solace and your sustenance. Never doubt your intuition or the guiding light that accompanies you. Remember that misfortune will arise as soon as you cut yourself off from your source!

Keywords to Complete the Interpretation

- Welcoming
- Charming
- Endearing
- Benevolent
- Blossoming
- Tender
- Delicate
- Generous
- Friendly
- Altruistic
- Compassionate
- Very receptive
- Great inner sensitivity
- Deep
- Simple, without artifice
- Not pretentious
- Devoted
- Sincere and frank
- Humble
- Hope
- Dreamer
- Innocent and candid

- Deep love
- Sensitive to beauty
- Ability to feel moved
- Born under a lucky star
- Lives according to their dreams
- Confidence in destiny
- Illuminated from the inside
- Purity of soul
- Spiritual
- Fertile imagination
- Poetry
- Music
- Virgin body, nudity
- Fertility
- Rhythm of nature
- Countryside, forest and wide-open spaces
- Agricultural land and gardens
- Pets
- Matriarchal and feminine values

- Idealistic
- Optimistic
- Pacifist
- Serene
- Seeks harmony
- Quality of life
- Lives in the present moment
- Genuine friendships
- Universal
- Soul number

- Dual intelligence (right and left brain)
- Visionary and intuitive
- Premonitions and forebodings
- Clairvoyance
- Astrology, numerology and tarot
- Symbols, language
- Mystery

Reverse Card:

- Meek
- Credulous and naive
- Vulnerable
- Weak
- Resigned
- Melancholic
- Desperate
- Uprooted
- Cold
- Sensitive to criticism
- Susceptible

- Blue flower and extreme sentimentality
- Unrealistic and dreamy
- Chimera and illusions
- Utopia
- False beliefs
- Unreasonable fears
- Easily disoriented
- Passive
- Runs away from work and responsibilities

- Weak in character
- Reckless
- Lack of spontaneity
- Lack of will and courage
- Female homosexuality

- Lies to avoid hurting others
- Puts his foot in his mouth
- Refuses to see himself as he is
- State of mind (sadness)

How to Integrate the Vibration of the Star

To do so, you must awaken your life force and seek the truth. Any parts of your personality that no longer serve you will then fall away, enabling you to regain your will to live. This phenomenon is known as the 'mirror effect'. To achieve this, your ego and pride must die, making way for a more awakened being in tune with the laws of nature and the divine. This will help you learn to value yourself. You will realise that it is impossible to please everyone, and that the judgements, failings and fears that plague your life are holding you back.

This well-being and happiness are contagious, and you will feel in your heart that now is the time to give back to others some of what you have received from life. You find your strength in love, and your soul's greatness leads you to want to brighten up the lives of others. Your path is marked by destiny's gifts and resonates with high ideals, indicating that you will succeed in realising them. While some lives are filled with pitfalls and suffering, yours is blessed with the guidance and protection of a guardian angel. Pray to him and talk to him — he will be delighted if you do — but above all, listen to what he has to say.

CHAPTER 18

THE MOON

The Moon archetype represents the world of emotions and the inner self. Associated with feminine principles, it highlights qualities such as sensitivity, gentleness and tenderness. It also connects us to our homeland, our roots, our ancestors, and the stories of our family history. Guided by the lunar cycle, the Moon card also symbolises motherhood and the deep bond between a mother and her child. Although it is often overlooked when it appears in a reading, the Moon is essential because it meets our most basic human needs for care, nurturing, warmth and unconditional love. In many ways, it is the miracle of life itself.

However, the Moon also has another side. It can point to unfulfilled dreams and disappointments. Like fog spreading over a landscape, confusion can set in, making it difficult to see the path forward. Moving from one disillusionment to another, a person may become susceptible to the negative influence of others, allowing themselves to be overwhelmed by dark and troubling thoughts. Fear rises, panic sets in and we lose direction. When that happens, our inner demons may take control and pull us towards despair, depression or even suicidal thoughts.

Nevertheless, the deeper message of this arcana is one of hope. It encourages us to break free from the conditioning that keeps us trapped, and to recognise the wider possibilities that exist beyond the veil of illusion.

Characters

A writer, a stay-at-home mother, a musician, a clairvoyant, a paediatrician, traditional professional, a midwife, a sailor, a restaurateur, an innkeeper, a hotelier, a waiter, a scriptwriter, a nurse and a soldier.

Personality

Qualities:

- Tender
- Sensitive and emotional
- Wears their heart on their sleeve
- Empathetic
- Warm
- Welcoming
- Compassionate
- Caregiver
- Great listening skills
- Introverted and passive listener
- Naive
- Simple
- Confuses dreams and reality
- Importance of sleep
- Feminine energy
- Close to nature
- It is beneficial for them to live near a stream
- Need for silence and long periods of rest to recharge
- Straight to the point
- Importance of family
- Likes to be surrounded by loved ones

- Humble
- Secret
- Reserved
- Original
- Talented writer and creator
- Poetic soul
- Born artist
- Ability to be moved and amazed
- Impressionable
- Follows the cycle of the seasons and the lunar cycle
- Sensitive to any form of rejection
- Able to read non-verbal cues
- Sixth sense
- Likes big parties and receptions
- Encourages family values and traditions
- Preserves and transmits ancestral knowledge
- Permanent contact with his inner being
- Rich inner life
- Exceptional gift of clairvoyance
- Prophetic visions
- Can remember most of their past lives
- Access to the Akashic Records

Faults:

- Melancholy and sad
- Depressive
- Hypochondriac
- Hypersensitive
- Angry and violent
- Frequent mood swings
- Blinded by her moods
- Strong tendency to dramatize
- Difficulty letting go of the past
- Influenceable
- Lack of self-confidence

- Authoritarian
- Defeatist
- Pessimistic
- Eternally dissatisfied
- Resigns from life
- Passive
- Blames everyone for their misfortunes
- Resentful
- Jealous and envious
- Whiny and plaintive
- Capricious
- Susceptible
- Anguish
- Obsessed
- Paranoid
- Illogical
- Takes everything literally
- Author of her own misfortunes

- Constant need for support and encouragement
- Impression of having been born at the wrong time, of being out of step with others
- Difficulty carving out a place in society
- Unable to face reality and its daily demands
- Fear of growing up
- Unable to take the necessary distance to have a fair view of things
- Goes from disillusion to disillusion
- Projects unrealized dreams onto others
- Life is made up of illusions and mirages
- Takes refuge in their dreams
- Alcoholism and drug addiction

Love Life:

- Romantic at heart
- Love occupies a central place in their life
- Fertile imagination
- Likes to brood and take care of their partner
- Sensitive to the needs of their loved one
- The relationship is a source of comfort and security
- They must feel supported, loved, protected and listened to
- Need for human warmth
- Needs to start a family to be fully happy
- Happiness lies in the simple things
- They appreciate everything that is usually taken for granted

Reverse Card in Relation to Love:

- Unstable
- Jealous
- Lack of confidence in their partner
- Envious
- Possessive
- Unfaithful
- Resentful
- Shy to excess
- Attraction to the opposite sex is purely physical
- Succumbs to their instincts
- Difficulty sharing life with a partner
- Fear of loving
- Believes they are constantly being used or manipulated
- Emptiness
- Anguish
- Lack of communication
- Conflicts of all kinds
- Loneliness

Professional Life:

- Creative
- Intuitive
- Human
- Versatile
- Difficulty working under pressure
- Needs to feel useful and brighten up the lives of others
- Needs time to assimilate and master the tasks to be accomplished
- Solitary
- Needs silence to work
- Night work
- Flexible hours and teleworking

Reverse Card in Relation to Career:

- Amorphous
- Night owl who has difficulty getting up at dawn
- Work isn't recognised or rewarding
- Works behind the scenes
- Lack of motivation and willpower
- Quits their job for fear of not being up to the task
- Difficulty finding your way
- Refusal to make sacrifices for work
- Keeps complaining
- Difficulty concentrating
- Unstable mood
- Overestimates their intellectual capacity
- Fear of change

Health:

- Risk of experiencing a large number of health problems

- Mental health disorders: depression, moodiness, cyclothymia, bipolar disorder, mood swings and schizophrenia

- Emotional disorders: phobias, paranoia and anxiety

- Eating disorders: bulimia, anorexia and obesity

- Alcohol and drugs

- Fragile stomach: ulcers and dyspepsia

- Liver cirrhosis

- Alzheimer's

- Allergies

- Chronic fatigue syndrome

- Insomnia

- Drugs, antidepressants and narcotics

- Dominated by their emotions

The Moon Applied to Your Daily Life

– You must respect your need for solitude. Make time for yourself regularly. Why not visit a lakeside cottage or take a daily walk in nature?

– You have a fertile imagination. Sign up for creative arts classes or join a theatre company.

– There is no point escaping to artificial paradises such as food, drugs or alcohol. Take charge of your life and make an effort to awaken the gifts and talents within you that are lying dormant.

– You spend your life waiting for others because you are afraid to take the plunge or make a mistake. You are an adult now and responsible for meeting your own needs.

- Who said life would always be easy? You are not the only person experiencing hardships. There's no point in feeling sorry for yourself or burying your head in the sand and hoping that your problems will magically disappear. Stop complaining and take the initiative to change what is lacking in your life.

- You tend to see everything in black and white, which can be self-sabotaging. Your paranoid mindset keeps you in a constant state of delusion and causes you to lose touch with reality. Try to see things as they are, free from emotion and judgement. Your life will be better for it.

- Many karmas follow you from life to life and are hard to get rid of. Consider taking a step back from your past lives to free yourself from the emotional baggage that continues to affect you in the present.

- Be spontaneous and stop opening doors to the past. By walking backwards or constantly looking over your shoulder, you risk missing out on your current life. Take the lead and get started!

- Whether you realise it or not, motherhood is part of your life plan, whether that involves giving birth to a baby, caring for an animal, or looking after an ageing parent. Your soul will grow when you take care of others.

- You are deeply attached to your family, ancestors and roots. Why not start researching your family tree or studying the migration of peoples, including your own genetic line?

- More than anyone else, you have a vivid imagination. Why not express this by writing a book, play or musical? A resounding success awaits you!

— You have highly developed psychic abilities. Life has blessed you with the gift of reading hearts and minds. Use this gift to heal or at least bring comfort to those in need. Your empathy is boundless, as are the qualities of your heart. You have the power to influence the course of events.

Keywords to Complete the Interpretation

- Caregiver
- Compassionate
- Good listening skills
- Tender and loving
- Human warmth
- Sense of family
- Community
- Surrounded and guided
- Versatile
- Imaginative
- Creative (painting, writing, music)
- Poetic soul
- Impressionable
- Wonder
- Sensitivity
- Emotional (repressed emotions)
- Need for solitude
- Reserved
- Sleep (alpha and theta waves)
- Restorative sleep
- Childhood
- Unconscious
- Young at heart
- Spirit of adventure
- Tenacious
- Water (live near water)
- Cycle (menstrual, lunar)
- Fetus
- Gestation, maternity
- Maternal archetype
- Genealogy, generation
- Past
- City, megalopolis
- Antiquity
- Right hemisphere
- Sublimation
- Psychic

- Secret
- Calm and unmoved
- Simple
- Spontaneous
- The night
- Dreaming and sleepwalking
- Hypnosis
- Intuition
- Vision
- Fortune Telling
- Memory
- Akasha

Reverse Card:

- Highly emotional
- Depressive
- Melancholy
- Motionless and passive
- Doubt of self and others
- Capricious
- Complaining
- Dissatisfied
- Jealous
- Envious
- Resentful
- Cowardly and fearful
- Passive
- Violent
- Susceptible
- Slanderous
- Drunkenness
- Sensitive to flattery
- Impressionable
- Disappointment
- Ambiguity: doesn't know what to stand for with others
- Tendency to dramatize
- Author of her own fears and her anxieties (too much imagination)
- Phobias
- Repression
- Flights from reality
- Illusion
- Refusal to grow up
- Routine
- Traditionalist
- Bewilderment

- Conspiracy
- Blackmail
- Delinquency
- Forgery
- Plagiarism
- Dishonesty
- Liar
- Cheater
- Sly
- Weird
- Extremist/fanatic
- Obsessed
- Perverse
- Fantasies
- Sensitive to flattery
- Whimsical and dreamy
- Trusts appearances
- Broken family
- Liaisons outside marriage
- Morbid temperament
- Contamination
- Infection
- Psychiatric and somatic disorders
- Alzheimer's
- Paranoia
- Alcoholism and drug addiction
- Cancer (disease)
- Superstition
- Mediumship
- Extravagant ideas

How to Integrate the Vibration of the Moon

In order to do so, you must reconnect with your early childhood experiences. The Moon reflects family bonds and ancestral roots, evoking a wide range of emotions, both positive and negative. It also awakens our creative spirit, inspiring us to express ourselves through music, art, writing, and crafts. The Moon belongs to the realm of subtlety and cannot be approached strictly logically. It is elusive, ever-changing and difficult to define. Above all, it represents the essential needs of the heart: love, connection, being listened to, a sense of belonging and warmth. When these needs are not met, our inner balance is disrupted and the stability of our emotional life is compromised.

Consider, for instance, a child who grows up without love or a mother's presence in their early years. They are likely to face significant challenges in adulthood. We have all experienced rejection, abandonment or a lack of love at some point in our lives. Healing begins when we release the weight of the past, especially when it becomes too heavy to carry forward. To do so, we must take control of our lives, even if it means rewriting certain chapters. We must also free ourselves from the fear of being judged and the belief that we are not good enough. We must silence our inner saboteur, which quietly destroys our happiness before it can take root.

Ultimately, the Moon teaches us the importance of loving and being loved, caring for others, and passing on what we have learnt so that the next generation may flourish. In this way, we use the past to build the future. The Moon also reminds us that life needs imagination and dreams. It encourages us to view things anew, explore other dimensions of reality, and embrace the inner richness we all possess. This treasure is infinite and waits patiently to be discovered and revealed.

CHAPTER 19

THE SUN

The Sun archetype signifies warmth, light, intelligence and love. More than any other arcana, it carries with it all the attributes of the soul that need to be manifested and brought to light. The Sun is enthusiastic and radiant, always moving and growing. It also symbolises the uniqueness of every creature and the innate human longing for freedom. Propelled by blind confidence and reckless faith, it follows a path guided by pure values. This is the path of nobility, where the soul understands the significance of everything after being enlightened by its penetrating vision.

However, despite its majestic character, the Sun can also be a trap. It occasionally expects something in return, such as honours, recognition or some sort of reward. In that case, his quest is subject to conditions. The Sun desires acknowledgement for its achievements. Many people fail at this stage because they are too distracted by pride, conceit, ambition and, most importantly, the ego — the sense of 'being' someone. This distorts reality, and the only way to overcome this is to view things with detachment and humility. In order to evolve, the entity must be sincere and motivated by pure intentions. It is through this acute vision that the Sun dispels illusions.

Characters

A child, an artist, a photographer, a teacher, a model, a daycare educator, a sports centre worker, a jeweller, a cardiologist, an interior decorator, a paediatrician, a senior civil servant, a public relations agent, an ambassador and someone in a good mood.

Personality

Qualities:

- Radiant, luminous aura
- Need for light
- Great vitality
- Energetic
- Passionate
- Courageous
- Smiling
- Welcoming
- Gold heart
- Benevolent, good
- Needs to share their emotions
- Compassion for human misery
- Prone to helping others
- Sincere
- Ability to turn the negative into the positive
- Takes life cautiously
- Clarity of judgement
- Transparent
- Integrated
- Leadership skills
- Guide, mentor
- Born to inspire
- Creative
- Colourful
- Avant-garde
- Original
- Stands out from the crowd

- Receives the confidence of his relatives
- Spreads love, peace, and harmony around him
- Great self-confidence
- Believes in his talents
- Good self-knowledge
- Likes to surprise and arouse curiosity
- Provocative
- Could know notoriety
- Great personal ambitions
- Guided by forces much greater than himself

Faults:

- Melodramatic sense of the theater
- Master of appearance
- Changes their mask depending on the circumstances
- Too emotional
- Low self-esteem
- Vain
- Pretentious
- Capricious
- Proud
- Condescending
- Wants to rule out any potential rivals
- Disproportionate ego
- Believes that others are at their service
- Easy to manipulate and manipulates others, too
- Emotional blackmail
- Seducer
- Fear of being alone
- Feels sorry for himself
- Lost touch with reality
- Hysterical
- Incoherent
- Aims for success and individual recognition

- Seeks to be the center of attention and to arouse admiration
- Trusts no one
- Individualistic

- Money, fame, and the desire to shine
- Sensitive to flattery and cheering

Love Life:

- Good
- Soft
- Generous
- Available
- Loyal
- Romantic
- Affectionate
- Likes to look good and be admired
- Joy for life
- Likes to have fun, to party
- Love is the engine of his existence

- Needs to share their emotions and feelings
- Makes efforts to keep the flame within a couple
- Fulfills their partner with little touches
- Prone to starting a family
- Nourishes friendships
- Importance of loved ones, whom they care about more than anything
- Meets the great love, the soul mate

Reverse Card in Relation to Love:

- Enchanting, seducer
- Smooth talker

- Doesn't know how to express his feelings

- Liar
- Domineering
- Overwhelming, suffocating
- Dishonest
- Exploits their partner's weaknesses
- Manipulator

- Has children with several partners
- Nymphomaniac, blinded by their primary instincts
- Divorced
- Latent homosexuality
- Prostitution

Professional Life:

- Keen intelligence
- Great capacity for discernment
- Professional
- Concern for perfection
- Workaholic
- Gives the best of himself in all circumstances
- Attracts the sympathy and admiration of colleagues

- Innate leadership qualities
- Defined by their social status, the position they occupy
- Employee or boss in high demand
- Acknowledgement
- Prosperity
- Spectacular success
- Creative

Reverse Card in Relation to Career:

- Inordinate importance given to appearance

- Patriarchal attitude, needs to control everything
- Important social situations

- Blinded by greed, promotions, and honours

- Employment that hinders personal development

- Doing it alone, not receiving any support

- Unrealistic ambitions, disappointments

- Sudden loss of social status

- Reckless acts that obstruct the achievement of professional goals

- Competitive spirit

- Proud

Health:

- Great vitality

- Morale of steel

- Excellent physical resistance

- Healthy lifestyle

- Takes great care of himself

- Importance of outdoor activities

- Subject to burns

- Cardiovascular disorders, high blood pressure with age

- Weaknesses of male reproductive organs (prostate, testes, inguinal, and scrotal hernias)

- Sensitive to lack of sunlight

The Sun Applied to Your Daily Life

- New perspectives open to you. Take your chance!

- Love will come into your life. Let your heart speak and savour these magical moments.

- We recognise your talent. You get a promotion.

— After the storm, the sun and good news will come into your life. A new cycle of happiness and joy begins.

— If you are already in a relationship, now is the time to formalise your commitment through marriage or an engagement.

— You have extraordinary creativity just waiting to be expressed. Arts, theatre, embroidery or haute couture — anything goes!

— You have the gift of making the eyes of distressed children shine. Use your teaching skills to help these young people reintegrate into the school system and give them hope for a better life.

— Your optimistic and enthusiastic nature attracts a lot of attention. Use your natural magnetism to inspire others and leave a legacy of a better world.

— You have become taciturn with the weight of the years. It would benefit you to reconnect with your inner child and enjoy life's simple pleasures.

— Certainly, life has blessed you with many talents, but be careful not to let your ego blind you. Come down off your pedestal and learn to embrace simplicity.

— Choosing between being and appearing will be your biggest challenge. Don't be fooled by trivial and meaningless things. You are worth much more than that!

— By trying to please others, you neglected your dreams and what was important to you. As you nurture your self-esteem, you will realise that you no longer need the approval or love of others at all costs.

— Just because your heart has been broken doesn't mean you should shut yourself away and mourn your miserable life. You were born to love and radiate joy. Pull yourself together!

Keywords to Complete the Interpretation

- Welcoming
- Benevolent, good
- Charitable, generous
- Human
- Nobility of heart
- Heart of gold
- Romantic
- Passionate
- Warm, affectionate
- Loves children
- Protector, good parent
- Fraternal
- Selfless
- Loyal
- Highly emotional
- Feelings
- Authentic
- Frank, sincere
- Courageous
- Proud
- Energetic
- Brilliant, superior intelligence
- Clarity of judgement
- Self-control
- Individual responsibility
- Leadership
- Power
- Guide, social role
- Inspiring
- Optimist
- Artistic, creative
- Light
- Fireplace
- Travel to the south
- Sunbathing, rayon sun
- Shines, the heat that emanates
- Very sociable
- Contact with the public
- Eloquent
- Know-how
- Elegant, beauty in the gestures
- Stability

- Full of vitality
- Smiling
- Jovial, happy
- Eternal child
- Curious
- Free
- Blossoming
- Opens their heart to others
- Happiness
- Harmony
- Peace
- Heart
- Compassion
- High self-esteem
- Unwavering self-confidence
- Self-knowledge

- Financial ease
- Likes to be admired
- Talents, gifts
- Male archetype
- Will
- Need for a higher ideal, sense of destiny
- Become the real you and realise your true self
- Meditates to calm their nervousness
- Life
- Centre of being
- Spiritual clarity
- The spirit, the divinity within

Reverse Card:

- Self-centred
- Individualistic
- Suspicious
- Susceptible
- Capricious
- Very nervous
- Hyperemotional, tearful

- Full of himself
- Inflated ego
- Great personal ambitions
- Eternal child
- Easily impressionable
- Great nervousness
- Vanity

<table>
<tr><td>

- Dramatizes events
- Melodramatic
- Feels sorry for himself
- Regrets
- Defeatist
- Manipulator
- Bluffer, concealer
- Mask, deceptive facade
- Appearances
- Irritable
- Angry
- Despotic, authoritarian, tyrannical
- Taste of power

</td><td>

- Pride
- Self-love
- Pretentious
- Wants to dazzle
- Sensitive to flattery
- Seeks prestige
- Applause, adulation
- Shine, honours, glory
- Gold, luxury, grandiose house
- Cannot cope with failure
- Vitality
- Latent homosexuality
- Prostitution

</td></tr>
</table>

How to Integrate the Vibration of the Sun

To incorporate the vibration of the Sun into your life, you must first free the child within you that has been suppressed for too long. If you can smile, be spontaneous, marvel at everything and nothing, and display absolute confidence in life knowing that it takes care of you, then you will have learned the Sun's most beautiful lesson. The Sun is a giver of life and symbolises happiness, love, sharing, kindness and deep friendships. In short, it tells us that we shouldn't unnecessarily complicate our lives because it's pointless. Instead, it invites us to find joy in simplicity and take time to savour life's little daily pleasures.

The Sun also shows that happiness is not found outside of ourselves, as we have been led to believe. This pursuit only destabilises us emotionally and strengthens our feelings of loneliness. Happiness is found within. When we start to prioritise being over appearing, humility over pride, self-love over feelings of inferiority, mutual aid over jealousy and contemplation over incessant activity, we adopt the most beautiful qualities that characterise the path of the Sun. A symbol of God, the Sun represents embodied wisdom and clairvoyance. It is by developing the qualities of the heart that we can draw closer to Him.

CHAPTER 20

THE JUDGEMENT

The Judgement archetype symbolises the realisations required to break free from illusions, beliefs and conditioning, and finally live in the present moment as oneself. Once this has been achieved, it is no longer possible to escape from oneself or delay internal development. Therefore, we must turn off all external distractions and truly embody our thoughts, words and deeds. To reveal the finest qualities of the soul, we must also erase the past completely and relinquish anything that no longer serves a divine purpose. Peace and constructive change will ensue as a result of letting go.

However, Judgement may also represent apprehension of change and the factors hindering the achievement of one's destined purpose. As we transition from one disillusionment to another, we gradually lose our uniqueness and become absorbed into the masses. Even worse, we gradually sever the special connection that binds our physical existence to our soul. Unable to distinguish between truth and falsehood, we place excessive significance on trivial and meaningless things that do not contribute to our inner growth. Distracted from our true selves, we create a reality identical to the mirage we once envisioned. If we continue to take pleasure in this sterile state, this wandering will persist and the lightning will not come to 'awaken' this sleeping spirit.

Characters

An inventor, a lecturer, a scientist, a clairvoyant, a politician, an internet celebrity, a baby, a progressive thinker, a computer, a communications director, a counsellor, someone starting a new life, someone following the call of their soul.

Personality

Qualities:

- Sociable
- Attracted to people, the public
- Charismatic, magnetic
- Enthusiastic
- Dynamic
- Passionate
- Spontaneous
- Original
- Humble
- Indulgent
- Understanding
- Diplomat
- Reckless faith in life
- Courageous, great endurance to overcome hardships
- At the heart of the action
- Desire for freedom, independence
- Fame, notoriety
- Predominant 'Yi' energy
- Awakening of consciousness
- Master, spiritual guide
- Mysterious nature
- Importance of daily prayer

- Popular with friends
- Needs to feel appreciated
- Very sensitive
- Taste for the arts, music, colours, and yoga
- Great soul
- High moral sense
- Consciousness guided by the heart
- Pure intentions
- Great know-how
- Great ability to persuade
- Gifts (clairvoyance, magic, healing, prophecy, vision, and intuition)
- Need for silence to come into contact with one's divine essence
- Connected directly to the Source of all life, to the soul
- Openness to universal consciousness, spirituality, and direct communication with the higher spheres
- Penchant for divination (Tarot, astrology, numerology, etc.)
- Curious
- Brilliant, above-average intelligence

Faults:

- Difficult to approach
- Difficulty communicating
- Egocentric
- Pretentious
- Condescending
- No one escapes their judgement
- Stingy with compliments
- Mysterious
- Fanatic
- Thinks he has the truth
- Materialist
- Wants to profit from everything they do
- Greatly misunderstood

- Resentful
- Boiling
- Impetuous
- Nervous, restless, overexcited
- Unstable, struggles to stay still
- Constant need to be stimulated
- Extreme behavioural deviations
- Lack of weighting
- Needs to feel appreciated, to be recognised
- Seeks to attract attention
- Hermetic
- Inaccessible

- Afraid of emptiness, of being alone with oneself
- Unable to inhabit one's body
- Flees the silence
- Can feel deeply alone, apart from others
- Intelligence bordering on genius reinforces the feeling of loneliness
- Omnipotence syndrome
- Manipulator
- Is an actor, wears a mask
- Enlightened, sect guru

Love Life:

- Sentimental life under the sign of good humour and enthusiasm
- The key to success is discovery
- Doesn't like routine
- Communicative joy of living
- To win their heart, you have to become their friend
- Loyal

- Undemanding
- Friendly
- Sociable
- Enjoys social outings and activities that are out of the ordinary
- Likes to surround oneself with acquaintances and friends

- Needs to feel appreciated and supported by the loved one

- Strong and deep feelings

- Union with a partner who has the same values and the same long-term objectives

- Common mission to achieve

Reverse Card in Relation to Love:

- Difficulty relating to others, with loving

- Difficult to approach

- Asocial

- Cold, distant

- Jealous

- Possessive

- Soulless

- Self-centred, has little interest in those around them

- Sexual and gender incompatibility

- Sterility

Professional Life:

- Many talents

- Great intelligence

- Ease of communicating with a large audience

- Original

- Likes to think outside of the box

- Discoveries, inventions

- Advanced technologies

- Good manager

- Can occupy a prestigious position very early in their career

- Comfortable in professions that require a certain manual dexterity, good reflexes, and a lot of movement

- Available

- Available
- Ability to transmit knowledge

- Guided by their intuition, their inspiration

Reverse Card in Relation to Career:

- Tendency to get carried away over nothing
- Unable to function without being subjected to significant stress
- Loss of contact with reality, lack of perspective
- Difficulty delegating, trusting others
- Fanatic

- Difficulty letting go
- Judges others
- Sense of superiority conferred by deep erudition
- Ideas of grandeur, megalomania
- Difficulty taking orders, accepting change

Health:

- Excellent health
- Knows how to enjoy life's little pleasures
- Unusual energy
- Active
- Great physical endurance
- Hypersensitivity to noise (ear infection)

- Torticollis
- Lung disorders
- Rheumatism
- Ability to heal self
- Music therapy, chronotherapy, reflexology, mud baths and mineral salts, yoga, meditation

- Restless in the presence of noise
- Vertigo
- Vulnerable to stress
- Claustrophobia
- Chronic headache

The Judgement Applied to Your Daily Life

- Gone are the days when you felt completely lost. You have just discovered your true vocation. Now it's up to you to take the necessary steps to achieve it.

- Don't just follow the crowd anymore. It's time to shine a light on your talents. You were born to inspire and brighten people's lives. So, what are you waiting for?

- Forgiveness is the ultimate act of humility. You won't be able to grow or move forward until you lay the groundwork. Lighten your heart and take the weight off your shoulders by forgiving all those who have hurt you.

- Procrastination is a big flaw. Stop putting off the things you can do today.

- The sacred plays a crucial role in your life. Keep praying and giving thanks. Each act of love begets another. Love and compassion are stronger than anything!

- Even if you are naturally shy, you will eventually have to speak in public to share your wisdom with as many people as possible.

- Stop resisting the urges that push you to make big changes in your life. Listen to your inner voice instead of trying to rationalise everything.

    –   You are at a crossroads. One chapter of your life has just ended and another is beginning. Let the flow of life show you which direction to take.

    –   What is the meaning of your life? You are unique, and your soul has come to reveal the gifts and talents you possess in any field. Until you discover the force directing your life, you will feel lost.

    –   A shocking event has just happened, or is about to happen. Its purpose is to set the record straight, as you have been going against the 'programme' you set for yourself before you were born.

    –   You're an old soul. As the saying goes, 'Those who have been given much will be asked much.' Be the instigator of change. Help the ostrich to open its eyes and the deaf to hear. Everyone needs to evolve and improve in this life, without exception. It is an immutable law.

    –   You are your own worst enemy. Stop criticizing and denigrating others. The judgements you make about others reflect you. Your inner world is reflected in the outer world. It is a divine law. We attract what we are and what we refuse to see.

Keywords to Complete the Interpretation

- Active
- Dynamic
- Playful
- Enthusiastic
- Spontaneous
- Captivating
- Nobility
- Action
- Mission
- Mysterious journey
- Timeless
- Universal consciousness

- Magnetic
- Charismatic
- Gold heart
- Humble
- Understanding
- Indulgent
- High moral sense
- Diplomat
- Universal love
- Sociable
- Likes crowds and audiences
- Needs to feel appreciated
- Brilliant, great intellectual abilities
- Ingenious
- Exceptional originality
- Curious
- Release
- Independent, free
- Be apart from others
- Genius
- Tenacious, has the strength to continue on his way despite the hardships

- Awakening of consciousness
- Spiritual master
- Power of persuasion
- Magical influence
- Transcends the limits of the possible
- Spiritual energy
- Child of light
- Spiritual awakening
- Bond with God
- Pray
- Meditation
- Music
- Centred, sees the essential with the heart
- Feels things instantly
- Enlightened mind
- Inspired
- Intuitive
- Great receptivity
- High vibration
- Clairvoyant
- Visionary

- Feels alone
- Accomplishment
- Social role
- Notoriety, recognition
- Gives thanks

- Tarot, astrology
- Revelation
- Spontaneous, unexplained cures
- Unexpected karmic reward

Reverse Card:

- Difficult to approach
- Annoying, intrusive
- Pretentious
- Resentful
- Unstable
- Restless, nervous
- Impetuous, boiling
- Euphoric, excited
- Lack of weighting
- Thoughtless, inconsiderate
- Extrovert (to protect oneself)
- Actor, plays a role
- Need to feel appreciated
- Need to be recognised
- Poses a judgement (on oneself and others)

- His differences weigh on him
- Lack of ideal and moral sense
- Wants to profit from everything they do
- Materialist
- Inaccessible
- Indoctrination
- Hermeticism
- Fanaticism
- Exalted spirit
- Mental intoxication
- Manipulative
- Mystery
- Saviour syndrome
- Guru
- Illuminated

How to Integrate the Vibration of the Judgement

To integrate the vibration of Judgement, you must be willing to take risks and make a fresh start, as this arcana requires a new way of thinking and being. To do so, however, you must take authority over yourself, give your life a new direction and make the necessary adjustments, even if it means redefining yourself, either partially or completely. To do this, it is important to free yourself from the past, forgive and, above all, heal the emotional wounds you have accumulated over the years. Everyone has the right to happiness, and Judgement encourages you to stop deviating from your path and to stop hesitating and resisting.

The greatest gift offered by Judgement is therefore the freedom to be yourself. It is, in a sense, an opportunity to reconnect with your true self, your primary goals and your dreams, and to make them a reality. Whether this freedom comes in the form of a divine calling, an awakening or a realisation, the outcome will be the same: you will let go of illusions, emerge from obscurity and embrace the changes necessary to access another level of development. Judgement symbolises the bravery, resilience and tenacity of the human spirit. Its message is clear: you must become aware of who you are by silencing the distractions around you. Follow the call of your soul and embrace your uniqueness!

CHAPTER 21

THE WORLD

The World archetype embodies the aspiration to elevate oneself, achieve self-realisation and be in harmony with oneself. However, if the World can embody finality, in reality it is merely the end of a cycle within a specific space and time. Consequently, everything is an eternal restart, resulting in a wealth of experiences, heartfelt wisdom and merit accumulated by learning the various lessons life offers. The World represents the yearning found within us all to raise our awareness, improve ourselves, and, above all, accomplish remarkable things. It encourages us to indulge in life's pleasures and assume our rightful place in the universe. We must remember that we are spiritual entities having a human experience rather than human beings having a spiritual experience.

However, the archetype of the World can also signify an individual's inner emptiness and failure to value life when they constantly fail to recognise its offerings. In this scenario, there is a risk of succumbing to illusory securities and refusing to evolve. One of life's great lessons is that we must all learn from one another because we are all living manifestations of God. A creature lacking compassion is arrogant, cold, self-sufficient and superficial. By acknowledging the journey that remains and learning to escape the dominance of the ego, we will humbly realise that there is so much left to complete.

Characters

A model, socialite, tour guide, dancer, travel agent, foreign national, high-society figure, flight attendant, guidance counsellor, globetrotter, doctor, frontiersman, revolutionary and ambassador.

Personality

Qualities:

- Likes to travel and explore faraway lands

- Citizen of the world

- Sensitive to what is happening around the world

- Great adaptability

- Phenomenal intelligence

- Everything works for them

- Optimistic

- Love life

- Expressive, good communicator

- Creative, innovative

- Simple, refined, elegant

- Integrated

- Perfectionist, always doing his best

- Their motivation is beyond any material gratification

- Motivated by the acquisition of new knowledge

- Must free oneself from suffering and all earthly ties

- Qualities of the soul relating to freedom, spiritual maturity, openness of the heart, and universal harmony

- Discreet, does not try to get out of the fray, prefers to go unnoticed
- Filled with delicacy, generosity, compassion
- Embodies kindness
- Available, self-giving
- Great listening skills
- Wants to surpass oneself and brighten up other people's lives
- Motivated by the highest aspirations of the soul
- Passionate about human nature
- Leader in their field, position of power
- Seeks to reach the plenitude, the serenity of the moment, and the fusion with the Divine that is in him
- Ambitious
- Their mission is to beautify the world and make it better by participating in humanitarian works or by awakening individual consciousness to the call of the soul, to the achievement of an ideal of life
- Seeks to bathe unconditionally in the love of the entire universe

Faults:

- Pretentious, sufficient
- Proud
- Greedy
- Egocentric
- Haughty, superiority complex
- Enjoys judging others
- Lover of social events
- Refuses to listen to the advice of others
- Interprets any comment as a personal attack, makes a mountain out of nothing
- Must learn to put things into perspective

- Superficial
- Likes to dazzle, needs to be admired
- Seeks recognition, honour, and fame
- Gives too much importance to what others think of them
- Social climber
- Difficulty in inhabiting your body
- Chronic dissatisfaction
- Lack of initiative
- Has the impression of being constantly questioned
- Is not immune to setbacks or loneliness
- Does not handle failure very well, does not allow himself to make mistakes
- Needs to feel supervised and directed so as not to lose their bearings
- Must learn to put things into perspective
- Lives his existence without taking on great challenges
- Unable to appreciate the little pleasures that mark their path
- Completely 'disconnected,' does not live 'in' the world
- Anxious
- Lack of autonomy

Love Life:

- Only feels complete when one has met a soul mate, cosmic fusion
- This 'spiritual union' is the engine of his existence and gives him all meaning
- Egalitarian relationship
- Importance of communicating their moods
- Must be able to express oneself and manifest the depth of their feelings without fear of judgement or criticism

- Serious and honest in his relationships

- Imbued with warmth and kindness

- Needs tenderness, have a fulfilling married life

- Has a very rich inner life

- Very attentive to the needs of their partner

- Will take a husband, move to their country

- Friendship is very important to them

- Works ardently to weave a social network, a community, which will support them throughout their stay on Earth

Reverse Card in Relation to Love:

- The life of a couple is not among his priorities

- Unable to make a romantic relationship last

- Selfish, prevalence of personal pleasure

- Demanding towards his partner

- The fear of being alone encourages them to control all the actions of the loved one

- Excessively emotional

- Changing mood, take it with a grain of salt

- Difficulty sharing their moods

- Dialogue gives way to cries, insults, and vulgarity

- Unfaithful, seduction is a way of life

- Divorced

- Unable—or refuses—to have children

Professional Life:

- Does not choose his vocation lightly

- Seeks to combine knowledge, know-how, and interpersonal skills

- Excellent communicator

- Available, amendment

- Mature from an early age

- Their many skills make them a sought-after employee

- Achievement of their ambitions

- At the service of everyone, with a purely disinterested purpose

- Gives practical meaning to their passions and motivations

- Works hard to achieve the goal they have set for themselves and constantly surpasses themselves

- Achievements and honours

- Very clever

Reverse Card in Relation to Career:

- Victim of racism in the workplace

- Seeks attention, wants to please at all costs

- Projects that will never see the light of day

- Does not recognise their own limits

- Has little confidence in their means

- Poorly calculated business boom

- Condescending, snobbish

- Lack of recognition

- Professional advancement blocked or delayed

- Insurmountable obstacles that lead to a fortune setback

- Fear of falling short

Health:

- Long and happy life

- Great vitality, energy

- Needs to move constantly

- Beneficial physical exercise to soothe migraines, sciatica, existential anxieties, and pent-up anger

- Rheumatism and arthritis pain. The hot rays of the Sun may often be the best therapy

- Fragility of the reproductive system

- Deficient immune system

- Miscarriage, abortion

- Metastases or fibroids in the breasts, ovaries, or uterus, sometimes related to the refusal of their femininity

- Complication following vaccination

- Contamination by certain particularly virulent microbes and viruses

- Vulnerable to infections and epidemics

The World Applied to Your Daily Life

- By wanting to try everything without asking yourself the real questions, you have gone astray. Gather your scattered energies and find your uniqueness.

- A great period of joy, honour, and success is coming. Cherish these blessed moments in your existence.

- The fear of tomorrow paralyses you as much as the fear of success. Be fully aware of your own limits and then go beyond them.

- Happiness is cultivated on a daily basis and is found in all the little things around you. Stop for a few moments and contemplate the work of God in all its splendour.

– Human beings are one big family. Unite your voice with those of others and dare to initiate the changes you want to see take place.

– Do not be too intransigent towards yourself. Set realistic goals as well as personal goals. This is how you will reach your full potential and achieve great things.

– Get out of your comfort zone: go on a trip to a foreign country, learn another language, and take advantage of all the development possibilities available to you!

– Too often in your life, you have forgotten yourself. Why not reconnect with what your heart really desires? Because the greatest gift you can give yourself is to embrace the being you have become.

– A complete cycle of your life has just ended. You have reached a goal or taken a critical step in your development. Celebrate this great achievement!

– Time is on your side. You will realise that you are no longer 'fragmented' and that you are one with the universe. You are not the same person anymore, and you now know the role you came to play here on Earth.

– You have been able to embrace your complexity and measure your own limits. For this, you had to face your responsibilities and develop one of the greatest qualities there is: compassion.

– Your potential is endless. Be aware that sometimes you have sabotaged your life without your knowledge. Learn from your mistakes and share your immense wisdom with others. For more than anyone, the universe has bestowed on you the gift of abundance in all tBy trying to do everything without asking yourself the important questions, you have lost your way. Gather your scattered energies and embrace your uniqueness.

— A great period of joy, honour and success is approaching. Cherish these blessed moments in your life.

— The fear of tomorrow paralyses you as much as the fear of success. Be fully aware of your limits, and then surpass them.

— Happiness is cultivated daily and found in the little things around you. Take a few moments to contemplate the work of God in all its splendour.

— Human beings are one big family. Join forces with others and dare to initiate the changes you want to see take place.

— Do not be too intransigent with yourself. Set yourself realistic and personal goals. This is how you will reach your full potential and achieve great things!

— Get out of your comfort zone! Go on a trip to a foreign country, learn another language and take advantage of all the personal development opportunities available to you.

— Too often in your life, you have lost sight of yourself. Why not reconnect with what your heart really desires? The greatest gift you can give yourself is embracing the person you have become.

— A complete cycle of your life has just ended. You have achieved a goal or taken a significant step in your personal growth. Celebrate this great achievement!

— Time is on your side. You will realise that you are no longer 'fragmented' and that you are one with the universe. You are not the same person you were before, and you now understand the purpose of your life on Earth.

– You have embraced your complexity and recognised your limitations. To achieve this, you had to take responsibility and develop one of the greatest qualities: compassion.

– Your potential is endless. Be aware that you have sometimes sabotaged your life unwittingly. Learn from your mistakes and share your immense wisdom with others. Above all, the universe has bestowed upon you the gift of abundance in all things.

Keywords to Complete the Interpretation

- Accommodating, conciliating
- Noble character
- Caring, considerate
- Available to others
- Great listening skills
- Open-minded
- Generous
- Delicate, diplomat
- Know-how
- Sociable
- Honest, sincere
- Inspires confidence
- Leadership
- Good communicator
- Overview
- Ambitious, determined, persevering
- Perfectionist, meticulous, attention to detail
- Gives your best, do your best
- Assurance
- Favourable conditions, circumstances
- Success, social, and financial success
- Elite, reaches the top of the social ladder
- Summit
- 'To be able to'

- Optimistic
- Discreet
- Simple, doesn't complicate life
- Symbiotic love
- Magnet
- Charm, beauty
- Elegance, refinement
- Ease, radiance
- Expression
- Sensitivity
- Androgynous
- Art, creation, unpublished works
- Innovation
- Brilliant, intelligent
- Insightful
- Alertness
- Individual consciousness
- Freedom
- Knowledge, reason, logic
- Glory, summit
- Achievement, fullness, unity
- Concentration
- Needs to see higher and further than oneself
- Charities
- Beautify the world, make it better
- Spiritual maturity
- Serenity
- Responsiveness
- The soul, feelings, listening, spirituality
- Vibration of their whole being
- Osmosis
- Universal harmony
- Travelling abroad
- Happy people have no history
- Great adaptability
- Research, education, medicine

Reverse Card:

- Vanity, pride, pretension
- Haughty, superiority complex
- Does not live 'in' the world
- Feels lonely at the top

- Selfish, egocentric
- Narcissistic
- Superficial
- Likes to dazzle
- Socialite, snob
- Upstart, too ambitious
- Seeks success, recognition, honours
- Gives too much importance to details, excessive perfectionist, fixation
- Greedy
- Spender
- Stubborn mind, static
- Offensive, vulgar
- Uncompromising with oneself and others
- Moraliser, values, judgements
- Chronic dissatisfaction
- Amplifies events and their difficulties
- Thinks that the obstacles are insurmountable, that everything is at stake
- Unhappy
- Crisis
- Reversal of fortune
- Shabby, miserable life
- Lack of autonomy, does not take the initiative
- Needs to feel supervised, afraid of losing his bearings
- Does not live with failure, must learn to learn from this experience
- Feels weak, helpless, small in front of the mysteries of life
- Distracted, inattentive to the world around them

How to Integrate the Vibration of the World

To harmonise with the vibration of the world, you need to pause and reflect on what you have achieved, both for others and for yourself. At this point, there can be no more pretences. You must make sense of your life and avoid being swayed by your feelings or different external stimuli.

Embrace your inner light and let it illuminate your surroundings. Your soul invites you to achieve great things and leave your mark on the world by improving the lives of those around you. It encourages you to achieve your noble ideals by helping those who struggle to find themselves and are afraid to leave their illusory sense of security in order to progress.

The World signifies the peak of a life cycle. To reach this point, you must first embrace life with happiness and accept that you are a whole person. Then, you must confront your responsibilities and learn from the challenges that have arisen in your life. Gradually, your heart grows and you come to understand that it's not just about changing the other person; it's about transforming yourself. You must let go, stop trying to manage everything alone, and, most importantly, embrace something greater than yourself. You must learn to distinguish between dreams and reality, develop courage and resilience, and embrace the gifts and talents life has given you. The world symbolises the achievement of a masterpiece: you! Appreciate your transformation, celebrate what you have become and recognise that you are no longer the same person you were at the beginning of your journey. Savour your victory over your limitations, and recognise your place in the universe.

Peacefully observe that another cycle is taking shape in the distance, because nothing in this universe is static.

CHAPTER 22

THE FOOL

The Fool archetype encourages us to embrace the simple things in life. A bit of a bohemian, he approaches life without expecting anything in return. He lives in the eternal present, constantly exploring his identity. He disregards judgements, expectations and conditioning of any kind. His profound wisdom stems from his ability to embrace the unknown and accept that he is navigating a realm of perpetual transformation. Without aiming to achieve any particular outcome, he maintains a constant connection with everything around him. Like a child, he has the capacity to be moved and to find wonder in the little things in life. An adventurer and a seeker, he follows his soul's calling, which guides him towards his final encounter with his true self.

However, the Fool can also symbolise a soul that has wandered through life's complexities. Swayed and tossed about by the winds, their principles are barely grounded. Consequently, the Fool fears uncertainty, risks and the potential dangers of the unknown. When his freedom is limited, he experiences feelings of rejection and misunderstanding, and loses confidence in life and the people around him. Naïve and lacking in self-awareness, he chooses to go along with the crowd instead of reflecting on his own thoughts. He sees himself as a victim of destiny, even though he is the author of his own story, and he dwells constantly on past events. His personal development is at risk. Disheartened and disillusioned, he risks either falling into a prolonged state of depression or simply giving up on life.

Characters

A loner, a poet, a tourist guide, a psychiatrist, an explorer, a visionary, a nomad or a traveller, a child, a homeless person, a comedian, a humanitarian aid worker, a disabled person or a mystic.

Personality

Qualities:

- Bold
- Courageous
- Persevering
- Autonomous
- Rely only on oneself
- Life of the party
- In a happy mood
- Bohemian in nature
- Seeks freedom
- Has no ties
- Lives to travel
- Only the school of life matters to them
- Open-minded
- In search of the absolute
- Their mission is to raise awareness
- Represents madness and wisdom, the visible and the invisible, the possible and the impossible, the alpha and the omega

- Spontaneous
- Original, marginal
- Unclassifiable
- Likes to think outside the box
- Avant-garde
- Mysterious
- Dreamer
- Brittle
- Sincere
- Wears their heart on their sleeve
- Ingenious
- Remarkable spirit of innovation
- Scholar
- High vibrational energy
- Bearer of infused science
- Altered states of consciousness
- Great visionary
- Amazing psychic abilities
- Driven by instinct and intuition
- Dedicated to achieving its objectives
- Challenges the established order
- Freed from dogmas and conditioning
- Loneliness, introspection, silence
- Empathetic
- Ability to capture the vibrations of their surroundings, to feel what is happening in the world and within
- Ability to come into contact with the deceased
- Knows, guesses, sees, and feels things

Faults:

- Irresponsible
- Carefree
- Nonchalant
- Paranoid
- Mistrustful
- Vulnerable

- Messy
- Unpredictable
- Unstable
- Restless, feverish
- Impulsive
- Lack of discernment
- Does not know how to distinguish the useful from the futile
- Lack of perspective and direction
- Excessive individualist
- Provocative
- Susceptible
- Full of resentment
- Unable to admit wrongs
- Lack of self-confidence
- Ignores who they are
- Sly
- Hypocritical
- Disconnected from their inner source
- Uncertain
- Without ambition
- Avoids all responsibility
- Lazy
- Rebel
- Revolt against authority
- Unreasonable fear of the future
- Victim of rejection and prejudice
- Carries the weight of life alone
- Disillusioned
- Tormented
- Strong tendency to depression
- Subject to mental illness
- Hanging out in the streets: beggar, tramp, homeless
- Internal tugging, maintains a permanent delusional state

Love Life:

- Premeditated romantic encounters
- Great need for solitude
- Likes to explore distant lands

- Mutual respect for differences
- Provides many tiny affections to everyone around him
- Accomplishes through the selfless giving of himself
- Idealist
- Thirst for freedom

- Often finds love while travelling
- True love can take years to manifest
- Tends to befriend people who are detached from any commitment

Reverse Card in Relation to Love:

- The sentimental field doesn't come easily to them
- Frivolous
- Carefree
- Impulsive
- Does not want to be held accountable by anyone
- Refuses to commit
- Extreme taste for freedom and independence
- Rejects any constraint or sentimental obligation
- Lies, betrayal
- Hates to mother their partner
- No awareness of the harm they're doing

- Proud, never questions himself
- Avoids any form of dialogue
- Difficulty expressing emotions
- Immature of heart
- Unable to satisfy their partner on a sentimental level
- Spends little effort on the viability of the couple
- Frequent absences from home
- They rarely get married or have children
- Experiences many romantic breakups

- Embarks on a new soulless adventure as soon as a relationship ends

- Elusive
- Unfaithful

Professional Life:

- Entrepreneurial skills
- Ambitious
- Very curious
- Workaholic
- Has brilliant ideas
- Always looking for new challenges
- Loves what is concrete, down to earth
- Seeks change
- Likes to move, travel
- Seeks to rise socially
- Seeks to surpass himself

- Bohemian
- Unpredictable
- Goes where the wind takes him
- Never has a stable job
- Out of the ordinary, original
- Individualistic
- Seeks freedom, independence
- Doesn't like routine
- Likes to organise their own schedule
- Embraces the unknown

Reverse Card in Relation to Career:

- Scattered because they devote their energies to a thousand and one projects
- Lack of discipline

- Bad career choices
- Unable to take responsibility
- Carefree
- Depressed, feels useless

- Nebulous future, without plans or guidelines
- Difficulty staying in one place
- Refuses to admit their faults and weaknesses

- Everything is constantly to be redone, no consistency
- Frequent delays, high absenteeism
- Acts on a whim, impulsive

Health:

- Hyperemotional
- Easily upset by the vagaries of life
- Sensitive to anything toxic
- Allergies
- Fragile nervous system
- Turns to alcohol, drugs, and narcotics to allay their anxieties
- Subject to mental illness
- Depressive states
- Sleepwalking
- Claustrophobia

- Parkinson's
- Alzheimer's
- General anaesthesia not recommended
- Takes very little care of himself
- Used to taking risks and getting into dangerous situations
- Doesn't listen to the alarms sent by the body
- Schizophrenia

The Fool Applied to Your Daily Life

- You are disillusioned with life. It's time to break free from all conditioning and take the plunge. Learn to discover who you really are.

- You took the wrong path. Your technical training does little to nourish your deep aspirations. Embrace the new spirituality emerging around you and indulge in activities that nourish your soul, such as meditation, yoga and prayer.

— You have the soul of a missionary. Embrace the unknown and go wherever life takes you. There is so much love to share, so many grieving people to console and so many people to heal.

— Cultivate your originality and creativity. You have an extraordinary vision of things. Let your genius express itself and ignore what people say.

— Stop seeing yourself as a victim. It's time to take your rightful place and leave the past behind. Life is short. Make the most of it.

— The weight of everyday life has made you lose your magic and the sparkle in your eyes. Reconnect with your inner child: sing, dance and scream at the top of your lungs. Uncover the happiness buried deep within you that just wants to come out.

— The greatest sages in the world know how to laugh at themselves. Stop taking yourself too seriously and trying to justify a life filled with pitfalls. The secret to happiness lies in simplicity. Get your life in order and focus only on the things that are worth it.

— Whether you like it or not, you have the soul of a gypsy. You create your life path with every thought and emotion you have every day. Your path is not set out in advance. Realise that you are already what you will become.

— No matter what you're doing, follow your heart. The heart is the compass of the soul and it is never wrong!

— You can choose a life of denial, illusions, mirages and lies, or you can be true to yourself and live a fulfilling life full of all kinds of opportunities. You choose!

— There is no such thing as certainty in this world. Your life can change dramatically in the space of a few moments. Have faith in life and don't be afraid to take risks to achieve your dreams.

— Freedom is your greatest gift and detachment your greatest quality. Your mission is, of course, to inspire, but above all, it is to show others that living in the serenity of the moment is the apotheosis of a successful life! Embrace the divine pleasure of being yourself!

Keywords to Complete the Interpretation

- Benevolent
- Pacifist
- Life of the party
- Enthusiastic
- Autonomous
- Ability to carry the burden alone
- On their own
- Strong in adversity
- Revolutionary
- Avant-garde
- Thinks out of the box
- Follows parallel paths

- Travels abroad
- Frequent moves
- Taste of the unknown
- Free
- Dreamer
- Brittle
- Born before their time
- Little empathy for his peers
- Absolute
- All at the same time, all or nothing
- Possible and impossible
- Real and unreal

- Lives on the fringes of society
- Open-minded
- Different, marginal
- Original, unpublished
- Strange
- Enigmatic, mysterious
- Undefinable
- Has the courage of their opinions
- Determined, decided
- Bold
- Not scared of anything
- Ingenious, innovative
- Versatile
- Extravagant
- Spontaneous
- Great ability to detach
- Intangible
- Adventurer
- Elsewhere
- Leaves their native land, lives abroad
- End of a cycle
- Visible and invisible
- Known and unknown
- Beginning and end
- Madness and wisdom
- Feel, understand, and listen to others, the universe, and himself
- Instinctive, intuitive
- Paranormal, parapsychic
- Clairvoyant
- Visionary
- Telepathy
- Altered states of consciousness
- Contact with the deceased
- The other side of the mirror
- Afterlife, beyond
- Wants to understand the mysteries
- Master of the universe
- Posthumous recognition
- Conclusion of the Creator's work

Reverse Card:

- Attached to their freedom, their independence
- Individualistic
- Difficulty recognising one's faults
- Does not feel remorse
- Stubborn
- Susceptible
- Messy
- Provocative, taste for scandal
- Indiscreet
- Restless, feverish
- Impulsive
- Unpredictable, lack of direction
- Thoughtless, foolish, irrational
- Carefree, nonchalant
- Irresponsible, careless
- Hypocrite, sneaky
- Duplicity, betrayal
- Lack of self-confidence
- Automaton
- Innocent
- Lazy
- Avoids all responsibility
- Social and material instability
- Vengeful
- Rebel
- Mistrustful
- Tramp, homeless, beggar
- Poor-minded
- Inner duality
- Uncertainty
- Materialist, refuses any form of elevation
- Without ambition
- Lets himself be rocked according to events
- Vulnerable
- Stuck in the human dimension
- Unconsciousness
- Illusion
- No contact with what surrounds them
- Ignores who they are
- Periods of intense loneliness

- Strange behaviour
- Poor physical health
- Discouraged
- Disillusioned
- Depressive
- Mental illness (alienation, madness, imbalance)
- Tormented
- Loneliness
- Periods when nothing makes sense anymore
- Carries their burden alone
- Carries the burden of the world
- Apocalypse
- Leak
- Progressive shutdown
- Plays the Saviour God
- Fear of the future

How to Integrate the Vibration of the Fool

To connect with the vibration of the Fool, you must listen to the call of your heart and soul. At this stage in your life, something new is about to come in — maybe a new cycle, a new person, or a new beginning. The Fool is embarking on a journey of self-discovery, carrying all his past experiences with him. However, these are only helpful if they help him to stay grounded in the present moment. The Fool does not want to follow a predetermined path. This would interfere with the freedom he values so highly, as well as preventing him from listening to his remarkable intuition, which drives him to follow all his spontaneous impulses. The Fool doesn't expect anything special, but he knows that anything is possible. He has walked this path of life many times before. His real goal now is to break free from the mental limits he has placed on himself, stop going around in circles and push his boundaries further. He needs to ask himself the right questions and avoid the things that prevent him from reaching his final destination. Like an upward spiral, he must become his best self and break free from the cycle of being reborn again and again.

The Fool's road is often lonely and full of karmic lessons from past lives, but it leads to wisdom. The Fool never looks back to see if anyone is following him because he is moving away from people to get closer to something greater: God. His destiny makes him a guide and a beacon, illuminating the lives of those who have lost their way and showing those who have fallen and chosen a life of suffering the way forward. Having him in your life can help you find your own freedom, too!

READINGS
AND
SPREADS

TAROT SPREADS FOR BEGINNERS

The final chapter of this book introduces you to the various types of Tarot spread, depending on the questions you have or the initial problem you wish to address. Some spreads provide a 'yes' or 'no' answer to your questions, while others help you to understand your innermost feelings. The rest cover the current year and the things you are going through. These sample spreads have been simplified to make them easier for you to understand and use.

1. The Card of the Day Spread

Every morning after waking up, take a moment to draw a card. This card will reflect the energy of the day ahead. Trust your intuition to guide you or refer to the description of the arcana in the corresponding chapter. For this practice, it's best to focus on the major arcana. If you're seeking further insight or need clarification, you can complete your interpretation by drawing a Minor Arcana card.

2. The 'Yes' or 'No' Spread

This spread is especially effective for answering closed questions that require a 'yes' or 'no' response. For this, rely solely on the Major Arcana. The outcome of your question will be interpreted as positive, negative or neutral based on the cards you draw.

Positive Answer	Neutral Answer	Negative Answer
The Magician	The High Priestess	The Hermit
The Empress	The Lover	The Hanged Man
The Emperor	The Justice	The Death
The Pope	The Wheel of Fortune	The Devil
The Chariot	The Temperance	The Tower
The Strength	The Judgement	The Moon
The Star		The Fool
The Sun		
The World		

3. The Cross Spread

This spread is in the shape of a diamond. You start by drawing four cards. The first card is labelled '1', and the next cards follow in numerical order: 2, 3 and 4. Place card 1 at the left point of the diamond, card 2 at the right point, card 3 at the top point and card 4 at the bottom point, closest to you. The sequence and numbering of the cards indicate the order in which they should be read; each card represents a different aspect of the reading.

1. Your current state of mind and what you should leave behind.
2. What you need to address and what could harm your project.
3. What you need to know: the desired objective and the various possible scenarios.
4. The answer to your question or the anticipated result.

4. The Monthly Spread

This spread is arranged in an uneven line resembling the shape of a tiara. For this spread, draw five cards. Start by placing the first card, labelled '1', directly in front of you. Place the second card a short distance to the left of the first, closer to you. The third card should be placed even nearer to you, between the first and second cards. Next, place the fourth card, labelled '4', to the right of the first card and perpendicular to '3'. Finally, position the fifth card, labelled '5', perpendicular to the second card at the end of the line on the right. Reading from left to right, your cards should be organized as follows: '2', '3', '1', '4', and '5'.

1. The atmosphere of the month in general
2. The first week of the month
3. The second week of the month
4. The third week of the month
5. The fourth week of the month

CONCLUSION

One evening, I received news that would change my life forever. My mother told me that my maternal grandmother, Alice Larcher Ménard, used to read tarot cards. She had been taught this skill throughout her life, but hadn't practised it in years. I later learned that she had made a promise to Saint Teresa to stop reading cards after the tragic loss of one of her sons.

Several years ago, however, my grandmother had used this God-given gift to support her family during a difficult time when three of her ten children were hospitalised. Without health insurance, which didn't exist back then, she accumulated debts and needed to find a way to make ends meet. The dozen or so people she housed relied on her, and her income was no longer sufficient to cover the enormous sums swallowed up by medical costs. Despite her vow to Saint Teresa, she decided to use her gift to obtain money, escape poverty, and feed her family.

I can still picture the way diamonds sparkled in my grandmother's piercing eyes — sometimes bluish grey, sometimes seafoam green — when I told her I wanted to learn card reading. Although her vow prevented her from practising it herself, it did not stop her from passing on her knowledge, and so she was able to teach me. If I recall correctly, it was 29 January 1991, just after my grandmother had celebrated her 85th birthday.

Alas, in May of that same year, my grandmother lost a fourth child. Exhausted from the struggle, she said, 'I can no longer see another of my children die.' She then passed away, much like an angel, to be reunited with the rest of her beloved family. My greatest regret is that I only had the opportunity to learn a few brief lessons under her guidance. This knowledge had been passed down orally from generation to generation.

However, almost four months after her death, my grandmother visited me in the middle of the night! What a wonderful gift of life! I realised then that, despite the torments of my teenage years, she was one of my guardian angels. She took me to her quaint hometown of Chénier in the Outaouais (Haute Gatineau) and showed me how she used to prepare 'meals' for her guests, as well as the places where she used to play and swing as a child. What I remember most is her zest for life and the simplicity of this very avant-garde woman for her time.

Before she left, she embraced me tightly. Then she took both my hands in hers, looked me straight in the eye and smiled broadly. My hands turned white as a sheet, and I could feel electric shocks travelling through my whole body. It seemed as if that moment stretched on for hours. Without knowing how, she had passed on all her knowledge — her gift to me — without uttering a single word.

Since that autumn evening in 1991, cards and tarot have started talking to me. However, it wasn't me who chose the cards; they chose me. The legacy of my maternal line and my ancestors, the 'card readers', still lives through me.

This book is the fruit of the intuitive knowledge passed on to me by my ancestors, which I have spent nearly 25 years perfecting. May He open the way to your heart and to true knowledge! The heart knows what the mind does not — this was the mission bestowed upon my grandmother, and it is now mine too.

APPENDIX

TABLE I:
Tarot and Astrological Correspondence

Major Arcanas	Signs	Planets
I- The Magician	Aries	Mercury
II- The High Priestess		Moon
III- The Empress	Virgo	Mercury and Venus
IV- The Emperor	Taurus	
V- The Pope		Jupiter
VI- The Lover	Gemini	
VII- The Chariot	Sagittarius	Mars and Jupiter
VIII- The Justice	Libra	
VIIII- The Hermit	Virgo and Capricorn	Saturn
X- The Wheel of Fortune		Mercury and Jupiter
XI- The Strength	Leo	Mars and Sun
XII- The Hanged	Pisces	

Man		
XIII- The Death	Scorpio	
XIIII- The Temperance	Libra and Aquarius	
XV- The Devil		Mars and Pluto
XVI- The Tower		Uranus
XVII- The Star	Aquarius	Venus and Neptune
XVIII- The Moon	Cancer	Moon and Neptune
XVIIII- The Sun	Leo	Mars and Sun
XX- The Judgement		Uranus and Pluto
XXI- The World		Jupiter
XXII- The Fool		Uranus and Neptune

TABLE II:

Astrological Correspondences

Minor Arcanas	Signs	Planets
Ace	Gemini and Virgo	Mercury
Two	Cancer	Moon
Three	Taurus and Libra	Venus
Four	Lion	Earth and Sun
Five	Aries	Mars
Six	Sagittarius	Jupiter
Seven	Capricorn	Saturn
Eight	Aquarius	Uranus
Nine	Pisces	Neptune
Ten	Scorpio	Pluto
Page	Gemini	Mercury
Knight	Aries	Mars
Queen	Taurus, Libra, and Cancer	Venus and Moon
King	Leo, Sagittarius, and Capricorn	Sun, Jupiter, and Saturn

Families	Signs	Elements
Wands	Aries/Leo/Sagittarius	Fire
Pentacles	Taurus/Virgo/Capricorn	Earth
Swords	Gemini/Libra/Aquarius	Air
Cups	Cancer/Scorpio/Pisces	Water

Table III

Correspondence of Minor Arcanas with Playing Cards

Ace of Wands	A ♦	Ace of Swords	A♠
Two of Wands	2♦	Two of Swords	2♠
Three of Wands	3♦	Three of Swords	3♠
Four of Wands	4♦	Four of Swords	4♠
Five of Wands	5♦	Five of Swords	5♠
Six of Wands	6♦	Six of Swords	6♠
Seven of Wands	7♦	Seven of Swords	7♠
Eight of Wands	8♦	Eight of Swords	8♠
Nine of Wands	9♦	Nine of Swords	9♠
Ten of Wands	10♦	Ten of Swords	10♠
Page of Wands	V♦	Page of Swords	V♠
Knight of Wands	-	Knight of Swords	-
Queen of Wands	Q♦	Queen of Swords	Q♠
King of Wands	R♦	King of Swords	R♠

Ace of Pentacles	A♣	Ace of Cups	A♥
Two of Pentacles	2♣	Two of Cups	2♥
Three of Pentacles	3♣	Three of Cups	3♥
Four of Pentacles	4♣	Four of Cups	4♥
Five of Pentacles	5♣	Five of Cups	5♥
Six of Pentacles	6♣	Six of Cups	6♥
Seven of Pentacles	7♣	Seven of Cups	7♥
Eight of Pentacles	8♣	Eight of Cups	8♥
Nine of Pentacles	9♣	Nine of Cups	9♥
Ten of Pentacles	10♣	Ten of Cups	10♥
Page of Pentacles	V♣	Page of Cups	V♥
Knight of Pentacles	-	Knight of Cups	-
Queen of Pentacles	Q♣	Queen of Cups	Q♥
King of Pentacles	R♣	King of Cups	R♥

BIOGRAPHY

Astrologer and clairvoyant, Yves Rochon has been writing, teaching, running workshops and providing private consultations for the past 20 years. He has also worked for over 22 years in the field of finance, in particular, for the Sisters of Charity of Ottawa (now Bruyere Continuing Care), as a second language teacher, as a federal government employee, and, finally, as a French Curriculum Developer, Editor and Translator for Oxford Learning.

Yves is a graduate in psychology, accounting, education and astrology and is currently completing a PhD in metaphysical sciences to further his knowledge in this field and share it with others. A conscientious guide, he humbly takes it upon himself to help people perceive their inner light by removing blockages and thought patterns that hinder soul evolution. He has also always been passionate about karma and past lives.

He is also the author of the books *Les Secrets de Votre Destinée: Découvrez Votre Mission de Vie à Partir de Votre Date de Naissance* and *Le Tarot en un Clin d'Oeil*, published by Octave Publishing in 2012 and 2015 respectively. He is also the co-author of the bestseller *La Bible des Anges — Écrits Inspirés par les Anges la Lumière*, published in 2008 and with sales of over 125,000 copies to date.

REFERENCES AND SUGGESTED READING

Alexander, S. (2008). *The Only Tarot Book You'll Ever Need* (p. 184). Adams Media.

Bartlett, S. (2006). *La Bible du Tarot* (p. 400). Guy Trédaniel Éditeur.

Bunning, J. (1998). *Learning the Tarot: A Tarot Book for Beginners.* (p. 320). Weiser Books.

Dee, J. (2006). *Tarot* (p. 64). Paragon.

Echols, S. E., Mueller, R. E., & Thomson, S. A. (1996). *Spiritual Tarot: Seventy-Eight Paths to Personal Development* (p. 355). Avon Books.

Edward, P. (2008). *The Power of Time: Understanding the Cycles of Your Life's Path* (p. 208). Llewellyn Publications.

Fenton-Smith, P. (2007). *Tarot Masterclass.* (p. 342). Crows Nest, Inspired Living.

Garen, N. (1989). *Tarot Made Easy* (p. 383). Fireside Book.

Greer, M. K. (2002). *Tarot for Your Self: A Workbook for Personal Transformation* (p. 299). New Page Books.

Greer, M. K. (2008). *21 Ways to Read a Tarot Card* (p. 310). Llewellyn Publications.

Greer, M. K. (2009). *The Complete Book of Tarot Reversals* (p. 274). Llewellyn Publications.

Kenner, C. (2009). *Tarot for Writers* (p. 359). Llewellyn.

Macgregor, T., & Vega, P. (1998). *Power Tarot: More than 100 Spreads that Give Specific Answers to Your Most Important Questions* (p. 288). Fireside Book.

Pollack, R. (2007). *Seventy-Eight Degrees of Wisdom: A Tarot Journey to Self-Awareness* (p. 354). Weiser Books.

Quinn, P. (2009). *Tarot For Life: Reading The Cards for Everyday Guidance & Growth.* (p. 344). First Quest Editions.

White, D. (2009). *The Easiest Way to Learn the Tarot - Ever!* (p. 324). BookSurge Publishing.